W.B. Yeats

WORKS & DAYS

TREASURES FROM THE YEATS COLLECTION

WB Yeats

WORKS & DAYS

TREASURES FROM THE YEATS COLLECTION

*A book to accompany the Yeats Exhibition
at The National Library of Ireland 2006*

*James Quin (life), Éilís Ní Dhuibhne (editor),
Ciara McDonnell (picture research)*

First published in 2006 by
The National Library of Ireland
Kildare street, Dublin 2
www.nli.ie

Library of Congress Cataloging-in-Publication Data are available for this book.

A CIP catalogue record for this book is available from the British Library.

ISBN 0 907328 63 6 (hardback)
ISBN 0 907328 62 8 (paperback)

Designer: Nicole McKenna
Copy-editor: Alicia McAuley
Production: Wordwell Ltd

Printed by Castuera, Pamplona

WHEN YOU ARE OLD

When you are old and grey and full of sleep,

And nodding by the fire, take down this book,

And slowly read, and dream of the soft look

Your eyes had once, and of their shadows deep;

How many loved your moments of glad grace,

And loved your beauty with love false or true,

But one man loved the pilgrim soul in you,

And loved the sorrows of your changing face;

And bending down beside the glowing bars,

Murmur, a little sadly, how Love fled

And paced upon the mountains overhead

And hid his face among a crowd of stars.

CONTENTS:

DIRECTOR'S PREFACE

Since Mrs George Yeats donated a first edition of her husband's earliest collection of poems, *The wanderings of Oisin and other poems*, to the National Library in 1939, the Library has continued to benefit from the generosity of the Yeats family. Thanks to their munificence, the National Library's collection is now the largest in the world and is one of the main sources for researchers investigating Yeats and his work. It is also without question one of Ireland's most important cultural treasures.

Extensive research on the Yeats Collection in the National Library has been carried out in preparation for the major exhibition on the poet that opened in the summer of 2006. Some of the information assembled in connection with the Exhibition, and a delightful selection of images used in it, have been brought together in this book, which has been designed as a companion to and memento of the Yeats Exhibition.

Very many people helped in one way or another with the Exhibition's preparation. We wish to express our gratitude to all of them. Apart from the dedicated exhibition staff—Catherine Fahy, Keeper of Special Programmes, Éilís Ní Dhuibhne, Ciara McDonnell, Luca Crispi and James Quin—there are many others in the National Library who played a crucial role in its preparation. These include the Keeper of Manuscripts, Gerard Lyne, and his staff—Elizabeth Kirwan, Jenny Doyle, Tom Desmond, Liam Ó Luanaigh, Stephen Quinn and Paul Jones. We would also like to thank our conservators Matthew Cains and Nicola Ralston, Sara Smyth of the National Photographic Archive, Joanna Finegan of the Prints and Drawings Department, Brian McKenna, Keeper of Systems, Jim O'Shea and Gerry Kavanagh from the IT section, Dónall Ó Luanaigh, Keeper of Collections, Gerry Long of the Printed Books Department, Colette Byrne, Keeper of Administration, and her staff—Gráinne Ní Néill, Margaret Toomey and in particular Mark Hardy—and lastly, Colette O'Flaherty of Education and Outreach.

David Monahan undertook the onerous task of doing the photography for the exhibition and for this book, and we are very grateful to him.

We would also like to thank two former members of staff who made a significant contribution to the exhibition: Peter Kenny, recently retired from the

Manuscripts Department and Katherine McSharry, former Exhibition Coordinator.

Several Yeats scholars have given us the benefit of their ideas and learning: we are particularly grateful to Professors Terence Brown, Roy Foster, Warwick Gould, Meg Harper, Declan Kiberd, Jim Mays, James Pethica, Ann Saddlemyer and Deirdre Toomey.

We would like to record a particular note of thanks to R.A. Gilbert, Stacey Herbert and Neil Mann, who gave us the benefit of their expertise in many areas, including some of the more esoteric and technical aspects of Yeats's work, and who contributed significantly to the texts and installations in the Exhibition.

Martello Media designed the Exhibition and produced the computer installations. We acknowledge the enthusiasm and creative energy of Mark Leslie, Carol Gleeson, Rob Reid, Peter Whittaker, Anne Patten and Iseult Ó Síocháin. Caoimhe Dunne, Fiona Daly, Aveen Holland and Cormac Figgis have made wonderful new artwork and original installations; Alan Gilsenan of Yellow Asylum has worked imaginatively with us on the production of films for the Exhibition.

Without the Yeats family, the Exhibition would have been impossible. We owe a huge debt of gratitude to Michael, Gráinne and Síle Yeats, who helped by loaning items from their personal collection along with their memories and advice, and of course by donating large parts of the Yeats Collection in the first place. For their true *flaithiúlacht* we are inexpressibly grateful.

But our greatest debt of gratitude must be reserved for Mrs George Yeats (1892–1965), who made the decision to donate her husband's papers to the National Library in 1959. Without that act of extraordinary generosity none of this could have taken place.

Tá súil againn go dtabharfaidh an leabhar beag seo léargas ar na seodanna luachmhara atá againn insan cartlann a bhaineann leis an mór-fhile Yeats.

We hope that this book will give readers some impression of the immense riches which are contained in the Yeats Collection.

Aongus Ó hAonghusa
Director
National Library of Ireland

FOREWORD

The words 'emblem' and 'image' recur in Yeats's poetry, and his life was marked by them. His imagination was governed not only by the written word but by intensely visualised epiphanies: significantly, he changed the title of his book of personal philosophy from *An alphabet* to *A vision*. The strength of the exhibition behind *Works and days* is that it has assembled a collection of objects, pictures, manuscripts and ephemera rich enough to reflect the astonishing vividness and diversity of its subject's life. Yeats himself would have wanted no less. He grew up surrounded by artists—above all, his incomparable father, whose portrait drawings and paintings recorded the generation of the Literary Revival. Throughout his life he befriended artists like AE, Althea Gyles, Thomas Sturge Moore, Edmund Dulac, Charles Shannon, Augustus John and Edward Gordon Craig, and he in turn inspired them—as shown by many items in the Yeats Exhibition, including a newly discovered portrait-drawing by Maud Gonne. His own fascination with visual art remained powerful, and in his philosophical and historical writings he constantly linked changes in historical consciousness to developments in artistic convention and technique. In some ways

Yeats remained the eternal art student and paid close attention to the way he was represented. Reviewing the portraits commissioned for the various volumes in his 1908 *Collected works*, he described the gallery of images as 'all the different personages that I have dreamt of being, but never had the time for'.

He still contrived time to fit more existences into one lifespan than any other artist one can think of. Yeats's biography will always raise problems of structure. How should we represent the life of a man who is simultaneously conducting an existence as poet, playwright, political agitator, journalist, theatre manager, lover and committee man, and who is capable of writing magnificent letters to different people on the same day, giving markedly varying accounts of his multiple activities? We have to try to see the life in the round, and to fight against the poet's own brilliant but retrospective pattern-making. For this, access to the widest possible range of material is essential; and this is why the National Library of Ireland is such an apposite place to review this heroic and protean existence.

The Library had been the background of Yeats's autodidactic youth; when he was nearly 70 he recalled:

I can remember myself sitting there at the age of twenty-six or twenty-seven looking with scorn at those bowed heads and busy eyes, or in futile revery listening to my own mind as if to the sounds in a sea shell.

The loyalty he felt to the institution, and the gratitude he retained for the librarian Thomas Lyster's early encouragement, has been magnificently repaid by the Yeats family. Their enormously generous gifts of Yeats materials are described elsewhere in this book. Over the years, these have built up into a unique repository, and the Library is the essential base for any serious study of the poet's work and life. Through the 67 years since his death, Yeats scholars have been met by George, Michael, Anne and Gráinne Yeats with unstinting courtesy and thoughtfulness; those of us who began labouring at the cliff-face some decades ago first encountered some of the material now in Kildare Street when it was still housed with the family, and have treasured memories of—for instance—reading Yeats's own books, with his own marginalia, in his own library, kept in its original order in his daughter's house. The survival of Yeats's personal library in the National Library, along with the huge treasure trove of manuscripts and the more recently donated occult material, is reflected in the richness of this year's exhibition.

But this creative assemblage of 'images' and 'emblems' also conveys the actual texture of the life as lived, especially the way he electrified people with his gift for friendship and collaboration (which contradicts simple-minded attempts to impose a retrospective psychological template upon his unique personality). It also illustrates the uncanny instinct he had for recognising moments of decisive historical importance and memorialising them in his art—from Parnell's funeral in 1891 through the *Playboy* riots, the 1916 Rising, the Civil War and the dislocations of the 1930s. The rich variation of his life is also reflected in his magnetic attraction to places of magical beauty: Sligo, Paris, Coole, Oxford, Ballylee, Rapallo, Penns in the Rocks, Roquebrune and finally Drumcliff. All these places are reflected in his poetic consciousness, as is his life among the most interesting people of his day. The Exhibition, and the book arising from it, do justice to this rich tapestry and to the artist who wove it. As he wrote in 1910:

A poet is by the very nature of things a man who lives with entire sincerity, or rather the better his poetry the more sincere his life; his life is an experiment in living and those that come after have a right to know it.

Roy Foster
Authorised biographer of W.B. Yeats.

INTRODUCTION

This book accompanies the Yeats Exhibition, which opened at the National Library of Ireland in summer 2006 to celebrate the work and life of Ireland's foremost poet. There have been other exhibitions on Yeats in various Irish institutions; the Library last mounted one in 1989 on the fiftieth anniversary of his death, but for several reasons a new major exhibition on Yeats is timely.

Most urgent is the desirability of acknowledging the debt owed to the Yeats family, who have donated to the National Library what is unquestionably one of the most important collections of Irish literary manuscripts. Thanks to their gift, the Yeats Collection at the National Library is the largest archive of Yeats manuscripts and books in the world. It is also one of Ireland's greatest cultural treasures. The main reason for holding a Yeats Exhibition now is simply to heighten public awareness of the Collection and to celebrate it in appropriate style.

A second reason is to showcase for the first time sections of the archive that have been acquired recently. The acquisition of the Yeats papers by the Library has been a protracted process. They have arrived in stages since Yeats's death in 1939. Mrs George Yeats, his widow, made her first donation to the National Library during that year, and in 1959 she decided that the Library would receive the entire Yeats Collection. During the 1960s the manuscripts of many of Yeats's poems and plays were handed over. In 1985, her son Michael Yeats and his wife Gráinne presented a further large cluster of papers, mainly consisting of working notes, notebooks and correspondence, including the correspondence of Yeats's father, John Butler Yeats. In 2000 and 2002, donations were made under the terms of the tax credit scheme (*Taxes Consolidation Act*, 1997, section 1003), including a very substantial assortment of manuscripts relating to the occult and Yeats's personal library—more than 3,000 volumes. Owing to the process of continuous acquisition over a long period, large sections of the Collection were not previously available for exhibition.

The material relating to the occult is a case in point. This forms a particularly valuable addition to sources for Yeatsian scholarship. It includes, most importantly, the 'automatic writing' carried out by George and Yeats after their marriage in 1917, which was a significant source of inspiration for his later poetry. It also includes many other manuscripts generated by his lifelong interest in the supernatural: descriptions of séances; accounts of visions and miracles; dream notebooks as well as much colourful paraphernalia employed in the rituals and magical activities of the esoteric societies of which he was a member, such as The Golden Dawn. The availability of this material fundamentally enlightens our understanding of Yeats's sources and ideas, and confirms that he was, in the words of his biographer Terence Brown:

a writer for whom magic, ritual and 'communication' with the dead and with spirits were profoundly experiential things which affected how he thought and felt about human life, about its passions and its meanings. (Brown 377)

This is an aspect of Yeats's disposition which, Brown adds, has been problematic for many scholars working in the humanist liberal tradition. The accession of the large collection of occult manuscripts to the National Library's holdings renders it impossible to dismiss or underestimate. Now that this particular section of the Yeats Collection has been conserved, catalogued and made available to researchers, a key motivation for the 2006 Exhibition is to display and highlight what is the most radical recent addition to the corpus of Yeats manuscripts.

Finally, a Yeats Exhibition is timely because the National Library now has a dedicated exhibition hall for the first time in its history. In 2004 an exhibition area was opened adjacent to the main library building on Kildare Street. The opening coincided with the centenary of Bloomsday—the day on which James Joyce's novel *Ulysses* is set; it was appropriate that the first exhibition focused on that work and on Ireland's most important novelist. It is equally fitting that the beautiful new space now be used to present an exhibition on our most important poet—Yeats.

The Exhibition

The structure of this exhibition is biographical. It presents a selection of manuscripts, books, photographs, paintings and artefacts designed to illustrate the journey of the 'pilgrim soul' of Yeats, the writer and the man, from his emergence as a poet in the 1880s to his death in 1939, by which time his work had already achieved canonical status.

Yeats lived a rich life. He belonged to a lively and artistic family—his father and brother were great painters, his sisters Susan (Lily) and Elizabeth (Lollie) were artists, craftswomen and designers. Manuscripts, publications and artefacts in the exhibition convey a sense of the immense creative energy which permeated his family—evident in items such as the *Ye Pleiades* manuscript, a home-made 'magazine' which included pictures by Jack and poems by W.B. and Lollie Yeats, and was bound and sewn by Lollie; or the rare journal *The Vegetarian*, to which W.B., Jack and Lollie Yeats all contributed in 1888 when they lived in Bedford Park in London.

From adolescence, Yeats was extremely sociable and as a young man quickly became involved in various groups—literary, political, and otherwise. In 1885, for example, he met Katharine Tynan, a young Dublin poet, and was introduced to the literary salon she held on Sundays in her father's house in Clondalkin. There he met the Dublin intelligentsia of the day, mostly members of the Contemporary Club, one of the first of the many societies Yeats was to join in his lifetime. Soon, he was also enrolled in the Young Ireland Society, had met the old Fenian John O'Leary, and became deeply interested in political and cultural nationalism. 'Through him I found my theme,' Yeats wrote of O'Leary, meaning that O'Leary had introduced him to ideas of Irishness which, for the first half of the poet's life in particular, were crucial to his own literary journey.

These were the first of the many societies to which Yeats would belong over the course of his life. Later, he would join organisations devoted to spiritualism and magic, to poetry and literature in general, and to the theatre. He founded or co-founded more than half a dozen organisations himself: the Dublin Hermetic Society (1885), the Rhymers' Club (1890), the Irish Literary Society (1892), the Irish National Theatre Society (1903), the Abbey Theatre (1904) and the Irish Academy of Letters (1932). Among the many societies of which he was a member, apart from those already mentioned, were the Theosophical Society, the Hermetic Order of the Golden Dawn, which he joined in 1890, the Irish Senate, to which he was nominated in 1922, immediately after the foundation of the Irish state—and, more ingloriously, the

Eugenics Society, which he joined in 1936. The Exhibition includes documents and photographs relating to all of these groups, and indicates that although Yeats might not have regarded himself as a luminary until he was a 'sixty year old smiling public man', his active involvement in public organisations began at an early stage in his life.

It is not surprising, given his sociability and interest in groups, that Yeats had a wide circle of friends. He expressed a yearning for an otherworld of one kind or another in many poems, such as 'The stolen child', and for a solitary life in some—most famously, 'The lake isle of Innisfree'. As a young man he liked solitary walks surrounded by nature and he even slept alone under the stars on occasion. In reality, however, his life probably included very few lonely evenings. His obsessive relationship with Maud Gonne is well known, and well documented by himself and others, but he had many other lovers, friends (and enemies), and eventually his own wife and family. In the Exhibition, the most significant people in the poet's life are represented by their manuscripts, books, articles, photographs or correspondence.

While the backbone of the Exhibition, and also the main subject of this book, is the story of Yeats's life, its most exciting aspect is the display of the original manuscripts of his poems, plays, and prose, and of his books.

The Library is fortunate to hold some of his juvenilia, including his two earliest known works. These were written when he was a boy of 17, living in Howth: the poem 'A flower has blossomed' and the play, *Vivien and time*. As David and Rosalind Clark put it:

'Vivien and Time' is Yeats's starting point. Here begins the great evolution of his total work, of which no step is irrelevant or unconnected. Not just the isolated greatness of particular works but the unity of all has pushed Yeats's reputation steadily upwards during this century. (Clarke 1)

Both this 'unity of all' and the mutability of Yeats's work are reflected in the selection of poems, plays and other works on display in the Exhibition, for which the concept of transformation has been inspiring. Yeats was a poet with a long writing career. His first poems were published in 1885, and he continued writing until he died in 1939, so his active writing life spanned almost 60 years. His poetry was always exciting.

This could not have happened if he had not continued to grow and develop, finding new techniques and new themes as he grew older. In his typically succinct and straightforward rhetorical style, he himself commented on one of the transformations he underwent as a writer, in a radio talk entitled, 'The growth of a poet', broadcast from Belfast by the BBC on Saint Patrick's Day, 1934:

When I was a young man poetry had become eloquent and elaborate. A generation came that wanted to be simple, and I wanted that more than anybody else. I went from cottage to cottage listening to old stories, to old songs. In my poetry I tried to keep to very simple emotions, to write the natural words, to write them in the natural order . . . In later life I was not satisfied with these simple emotions—though I tried, and still try, to put the natural words in the natural order. Modern thought is not simple.

In a view that has become an accepted tenet of Yeats criticism, T.S. Eliot, lecturing in the Abbey in 1940, pointed out that Yeats had renewed himself as a writer in middle age in a way which is exceptional (although he cited instances of this kind of literary rejuvenation in other great writers, naming Shakespeare and Dickens):

. . . he had to wait for a later maturity to find expression of early experience; and this makes him, I think, a unique and especially interesting poet.

Consider the early poem which is in every anthology, When you are old and grey and full of sleep, or A Dream of Death in the same volume of 1893. They are beautiful poems, but only craftsman's work, because one does not find in them the particularity which must provide the material for a general truth. By the time of the volume of 1904 there is a development visible in a very lovely poem, The Folly of Being Comforted, and in Adam's Curse; something is beginning to come through, and in beginning to speak as a particular man he is beginning to speak for man . . . But it is not fully evinced until the volume of 1914, in the violent and terrible epistle dedicatory of Responsibilities, with the great lines

Pardon that for a barren passion's sake,
Although I have come close on forty-nine
I have no child, I have nothing but a book
Nothing but that to prove your blood and mine.
(Eliot 251)

Eliot emphasised the transformation Yeats underwent as an artist in middle age, a transformation which many would localise to 1916 (the year of the Easter Rising, an event which changed Yeats's view of modern Ireland) and 1917 (the year of his marriage to Georgina Hyde-Lees), and a transformation upon which he comments poetically in his seminal poem, 'Easter 1916'. However, other critics comment upon aspects of unity in his poetic vision. Declan Kiberd, for instance, writing about 'Easter 1916', a poem which acted almost as a template for other postcolonial poets writing about revolutions, links this work to one of Yeats's earliest poems, 'The stolen child', particularly in that it combines the intensely personal, the 'particularity' that Eliot admired, with the political:

That is heaven's part. Our part,
To murmur name upon name
As a mother names her child,
When sleep at last has come
On limbs that had run wild . . .

The reference takes us back to the child stolen by the fairies from its rightful human mother, a child who departed solemn-eyed, like Pearse and MacDonagh. It can hardly be a coincidence that both lyrics chronicle the loss of young life and the distress of mourners left to carry on . . . For him the dead were all stolen children.
(Kiberd 114)

Manuscripts of these poems, and of many other poems and plays which will be familiar to many visitors as well as many which will perhaps not be familiar, have been chosen to demonstrate the literary journey of Yeats. The material ranges from his early days as a lyricist enthusiastically engaged with nature, mythology, the occult, and above all, love, and, in his own words, concerned with simple emotions, through the middle phases of his life when he was immersed in the world of drama and writing more critically about the realities of Ireland, to the latter part of his life—when, having made his name as a poet of emotion and simplicity, he gradually transformed his style and thought to become a great modernist poet, dealing in a very direct and personal way with complex philosophical, artistic, and political issues of universal significance.

What is the real purpose of any archive of literary manuscripts? The manuscripts in the Yeats Collection are not like the *Book of Kells*—beautiful works of art, nor are they like the *Book of the Dun Cow* or the *Yellow Book of Lecan*—manuscripts in which great works of literature were written down in the days before the printing press had been invented and which would not otherwise have survived. Yeats's manuscripts are seldom beautiful. Much more often they are the opposite—almost illegible, very untidy and sprinkled with misspellings. All his work, apart from some juvenilia and some items he decided not to release, has been published, so, as would be the case with most modern writers, the manuscripts have no serious function as a means of preserving it. Apart from the obvious sentimental or iconic value, which should not be underestimated, does an archive of this kind have anything important to add to the sum of our knowledge about the writer? Is it an expensive souvenir or something more useful?

There are some obvious answers. In the first place, an archive such as this one is important for biographers. While Yeats's literary work was mainly published in his lifetime, his correspondence, his notebooks, his diaries (fragmentary as they were) and the vast assortment of writings relating to the occult were not. The latter in particular have been important in emphasising the true significance to his writing of his interest in the occult. The sheer volume of the material indicates that this entire area was much more central to his thought than has been widely acknowledged, and that a close study of his extensive and intensive manuscripts on the occult is necessary for a full appreciation of his creativity.

Clearly items like these, in addition to the manuscripts of works which were not published, some of which are displayed in the Yeats Exhibition, are of obvious usefulness, especially so in the case of a great writer about whom we want to know everything.

Archivists and textual scholars would argue that the manuscripts of literary work which has been published also have an important function for scholars and researchers. In the part of the Yeats Exhibition labelled 'The creative process' we have attempted to demonstrate what this function is. The manuscripts reveal for instance that Yeats was a writer who revised his work constantly, continuing to rework some plays and poems for years, even after they had been first published or performed. For his play *The Countess Cathleen*, for instance, which is his most revised work, more than 50 drafts are extant. Twenty-one of these are in the National Library. A close examination of the drafts reveals how the writer worked, which elements of the poem or play were in place from the beginning and what he changed as he went along. In 'The creative process' a detailed analysis of the writer's drafting process is presented. Some key texts were chosen to show how a poem evolved from a brief note, sometimes in prose, through several drafts, until finally, through this process of trial, error and progression, the perfect poem was achieved.

The formation of collections is also demonstrated. One of Yeats's best collections, *The tower* (1929), has been examined, and the way in which Yeats arranged the poems in this book and in others is explained. We often encounter the poems of Yeats as single works, and read them in anthologies of Irish poets, or in school anthologies. Of course he wrote the poems singly, and usually published them initially as individual pieces in journals or newspapers, but he compiled his collections with a pattern in mind and intended each collection to be read sequentially, as you might read a novel.

Another important aspect of Yeats's artistic disposition, a part of his creative character, was his concern with the design of his books. In the display prepared and scripted by the bibliographical scholar Stacey Herbert, many of his finest books are displayed with information about the designers, artists and publishers with whom Yeats worked.

All in all, every item in the Yeats Collection adds something to our knowledge of his life, his thinking, feeling and the way he worked. In the Exhibition, a selection has been made with the ambition of conveying some impression of the individuality of this writer, and a sense of what it means to be a writer of genius.

In the Yeats Exhibition, the story of the poet's work, as represented in manuscripts, books and other publications, is complemented by the story of his life. It is not reasonable to separate the two. 'Days are where we live', Philip Larkin wrote, and while Yeats's work outlives his days, both days and works are presented in this exhibition as part of a creative continuum. Since the biography is the structure upon which the exhibition is based, it was decided to make it the heart of this book. Our sources are listed in the bibliography, but we would like to especially acknowledge our debt to Roy Foster, the authorised biographer of Yeats, whose two-volume biography *WB Yeats: a life* (Oxford, 1997, 2003) has been indispensable in developing the biographical elements of the exhibition and in compiling this book, designed to be a companion to the exhibition.

PART ONE: 1865–1888

A FLOWER HAS BLOSSOMED

Come away, O human child!

To the waters and the wild

With a faery, hand in hand,

For the world's more full of weeping than

you can understand.

THE STOLEN CHILD

1865

Birth of a poet

William Butler Yeats was born at 10.40 p.m. on Tuesday 13 June 1865 at George's Ville, Sandymount Avenue, Dublin. He was the first child of Susan (*née* Pollexfen) and John Butler Yeats. The doctor attending Susan Yeats declared the baby so strong that 'you could leave him out all night on the window sill and it would do him no harm'. The house in which he was born still stands today, though the address is now 5 Sandymount Avenue.

Subsequently Susan and John Yeats had five more children: Susan Mary (Lily, 1866), Elizabeth (Lollie, 1868), Robert (1870), John (Jack, 1871) and Jane (1875). Robert died just before his third birthday in March 1873, and Jane died when she was nine months old, in June 1876. The other four children lived into old age, and Yeats even survived a dangerous bout of scarlet fever, probably combined with tuberculosis, in 1870.

Susan Pollexfen
(WBY's mother)

Rev. William Yeats
(WBY's grandfather)

Jane Corbet Yeats
(WBY's grandmother)

Sandymount Castle

WBY as a baby
(drawn by his father)

John Butler Yeats

page three

A FLOWER HAS BLOSSOMED

1867

John Butler Yeats's new career as an artist

In 1867 John Butler Yeats gave up his law career in Dublin and went to London to study art. He had been called to the bar in January 1866 but made little impression as a barrister. He seems to have spent much of his time in court sketching those around him, and his sketches may even have got him into trouble. However, they came to the attention of Tom Hood, who offered to put him in touch with London magazine editors looking for illustrators. Impulsively, John Butler Yeats decided to quit the law and take up a career as an artist. Despite strong objections from his wife and her family, the Pollexfens, he sold the house at Sandymount. He moved his family to Sligo, where the Pollexfens lived, and set off for London, where he enrolled at Heatherley's Art School. At the end of July, Susan Yeats, who was pregnant with their third child and had Lily and Yeats in tow, arrived with her younger sister Isabella at 23 Fitzroy Road, London.

John Butler Yeats

Merville, home of the
Pollexfens in Sligo

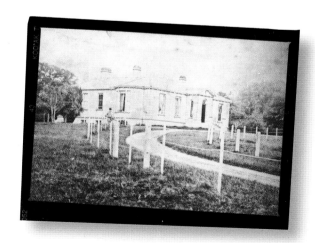

Jack B. Yeats

WBY aged ten
months with his nurse

WBY as a child.
Drawing by
John Butler Yeats

Lily and Lollie Yeats

1872–4

London and Sligo

Susan Yeats was dismissive of her husband's artistic life and friends, and hated London. John Butler Yeats's career as an artist showed no signs of profit, and income from his encumbered family estates was minimal. She often brought the children back to Ireland and during the 1860s their summer holidays in Sligo sometimes lasted until Christmas. Finally in July 1872 Susan Yeats took the children to stay at her parents' house, where they remained for more than two years. Living with their Pollexfen relatives, listening to the servants' stories, and wandering around the town and harbour were formative experiences for the Yeats children.

However, in October 1874, John Butler Yeats decided to move the family back to London in spite of his wife's objections, and in October 1874 they moved into 14 Edith Villas, West Kensington. Encouraged by their father, who thought they should get more fresh air, Lily and Yeats spent their time exploring London, walking from home to the National Gallery and back, drinking from fountains on the way and eating penny buns. Yeats sailed model boats on the Round Pond in Kensington Gardens, but both he and Lily missed Sligo, a place kept alive in their imagination by their mother's stories. Yeats's aunt Agnes Gorman summed up the difference between Sligo and London, telling him, 'You are going to London. Here [in Sligo] you are somebody. There you will be nobody at all.'

Elizabeth
Middleton
Pollexfen

WBY with uncle Fred Pollexfen in Sligo, 1872

William Pollexfen (WBY's grandfather)

Glencar Waterfall, County Sligo

1877

Godolphin School

On 26 January 1877, Yeats was enrolled at the Godolphin School, Iffley Road, Hammersmith. He found he had little in common with his classmates there, claiming later to recall saying to himself, 'If when I grow up I am as clever among grown-up men as I am among these boys, I shall be a famous man.' He described the school as 'an obscene, bullying place', and his friend Charles Veasey taught him to defend himself after someone called him a 'mad Irishman'. He was good at sports and won a cup for running in 1881, but his main interest was in science, and he won a prize for scientific knowledge when he was 13. His school reports show that he was not a good student, often coming bottom of the class, getting black marks for idleness, and being 'very poor in spelling'. Yeats remained at the Godolphin School until Easter 1881.

The other three children were taught at home by a governess, Martha Jowitt. According to Lily, she taught them to read and write, and was a stickler for tidiness. Lily also recalled the schoolroom in which they acted out plays while Martha Jowitt read her paper. Yeats, who joined them after school, took the acting very seriously, while young Jack pranced about in his mother's white boots.

A selection of WBY's school reports

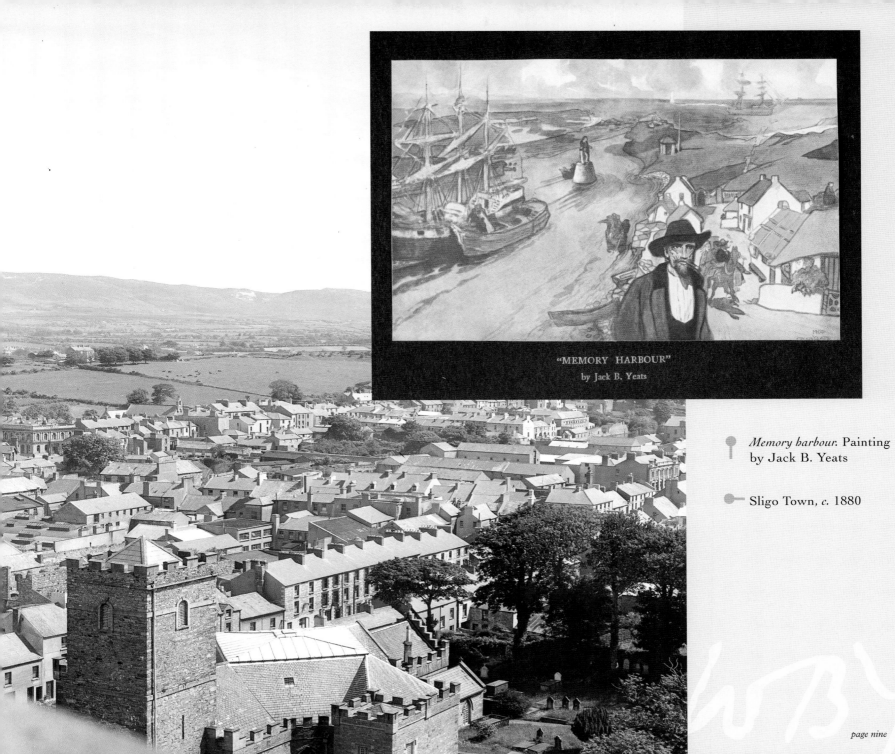

"MEMORY HARBOUR"
by Jack B. Yeats

Memory harbour. Painting by Jack B. Yeats

Sligo Town, *c.* 1880

1881

Howth

John Butler Yeats's chronic financial situation worsened in 1881 and he resolved to move back to Dublin, hoping for artistic and financial success there. Late in the autumn, the family arrived from London and stayed briefly at Leeson Street before settling at Balscadden Cottage in Howth. Lily recalled placing offerings of fish on the doorstep of their neighbour Samuel Ferguson, the writer, and she also recalled Yeats writing verse there. In 1882 they moved to Island View, on Harbour Road, Howth. The children enjoyed the years in Howth because it reminded them and their mother of Sligo.

With the family move to Howth, Yeats was enrolled at the Erasmus Smith High School on Harcourt Street, Dublin. He travelled into the city from Howth by train with his father each day, and lunched at his father's studio not far from the school. His fellow students included William Magee, who later wrote under the name John Eglinton, and Frederick Gregg, with whom he wrote a verse play. Another friend was Charles Johnston, with whom Yeats later developed his interests in the occult. Around this time his interest in science diminished and he 'began to play at being a sage, a magician or a poet' as he records it in *Autobiographies*.

Howth, *c.* 1880

Howth, *c.* 1880

Charles Johnston

A FLOWER HAS BLOSSOMED

Laura Armstrong

In autumn 1882 Yeats met a distant cousin, Laura Armstrong. Though she was three years older than him and already engaged to be married, he fell in love with her. In their letters they addressed each other as Clarin and Vivien, and she was the model for characters in his early plays *Vivien and time* and *The island of statues*, and for the character Margaret Leland in *John Sherman*. They had no further contact after she married Henry Byrne in September 1884. Yeats later recorded, 'I wrote her some bad poems and had more than one sleepless night through anger with her betrothed.' In a letter to Katharine Tynan in 1889, Yeats wrote that Maud Gonne reminded him of Laura Armstrong but 'without Laura's wild dash of half insane genius. Laura is to me always a pleasant memory she [*sic*] woke me from the metallic sleep of science and set me writing my first play.' He added, 'She interests me far more than Miss Gonne does and yet is only as a myth and symbol.'

Yeats was already writing poetry and drama at this time. The earliest poem in the National Library's collection, written on the back of a note to a Mrs Mary Cronin of Howth, dates from 1882, as does his first play, *Vivien and time.* Interestingly, the poem, which Yeats never published, seems to announce the birth of a poet—'A flower has blossomed'.

Laura Armstong

WBY, c. 1885

Terenure

In 1884 the family's still-declining fortunes forced them to move from Island View, Howth, to a terraced house at 10 Ashfield Terrace, off Harold's Cross Road in Terenure. The family would sit around a single lamp at night with Yeats murmuring his verses, and Lily remembered walking from home to art school in the city centre because there was no money for trams. Yeats's schoolfriend Charles Johnston claimed that 'The artistic spirit radiated out of everything in the house, sketches, pictures, books, and the perpetual themes of conversation.' He added that the house was 'full of generous impracticality'. Money remained a problem and the family were plagued by butcher's bills. John Butler Yeats was even forced to write begging letters to his uncle Matt.

George Russell

In May 1884 Yeats enrolled at the Metropolitan School of Art. His contemporaries there included Dora Sigerson, with whom he would maintain contact, and who later married the publisher Clement Shorter, the first publisher of 'Easter 1916'. He was also friendly with George Sigerson and Oliver Sheppard, the sculptor who later made the statue of Cuchulain, chosen as a 1916 memorial for the General Post Office on Dublin's O'Connell Street.

Yeats's best friend at the art college, however, was George Russell. Both of them were interested in literature and the esoteric, and together they went in search of 'Odic forces' emanating from objects at the National Museum. However, they had their differences. While Yeats was interested in magic and hierarchies, Russell tended towards the mystical, and while Yeats involved himself in esoteric groups and organisations, Russell tended to remain an outsider. Both Yeats and Russell were very involved in political and cultural life in Ireland, and often quarrelled and disagreed. Russell wrote for various newspapers and magazines, signing himself AE (a corruption of *aeon*).

George Russell (AE).
Portrait by John Butler
Yeats

Winged horse. Painting by
George Russell (AE)

GEORGE WILLIAM RUSSELL (Æ)
By John B. Yeats

A.P. Sinnett's *Esoteric Buddhism*

In 1884 Yeats was introduced to a philosophy that would be a key influence on his thinking, namely Theosophy. Although the term was originally applied to mystical philosophies that aimed to achieve a direct intuitive or spiritual knowledge of God (and especially the works of Jacob Boehme), in the late nineteenth century Theosophy (with the capital letter) had become almost exclusively associated with Helena Petrovna Blavatsky's doctrines and the Theosophical Society she had helped to found. These teachings were declared as the essence of all religions, and 'the synthesis of science, religion, and philosophy', but were particularly based on Indian Vedanta and Tibetan Buddhism. A.P. Sinnett's book *Esoteric Buddhism* (1883) popularised Blavatsky's ideas hugely, being a lot more succinct and readable than her own writings. Yeats's aunt, Isabella Pollexfen Varley, sent him a copy of this book.

Sinnett was president of the London lodge of the Theosophical Society and a close associate of Helena Blavatsky, whom Yeats later met in May 1887. Reading Sinnett's book had a profound effect on Yeats and on his schoolfriend Charles Johnston, to whom he lent it. Together Yeats and Charles Johnston founded the Dublin Hermetic Society, and Yeats chaired its first meeting on 16 June 1885, days after his twentieth birthday. The Society published the *Irish Theosophist*, for which Yeats occasionally wrote articles.

Madame Blavatsky

WBY, 1886. Drawing
by John Butler Yeats
(opposite)

1885

First published poems

The first known publication by Yeats was in the March 1885 issue of the *Dublin University Review*, where 'Song of the faeries' and 'Voices' appeared. 'Voices' had originally been part of his early play *The island of statues*, and was revised later to become 'The cloak, the boat, and the shoes'. The *Dublin University Review* was edited by Charles Hubert Oldham and in it, between March 1885 and December 1886, Yeats published 11 poems, three longer dramatic poems and an article on Samuel Ferguson. Oldham, who had rooms at Trinity College, had organised a group of intellectuals around the *Dublin University Review* and the Contemporary Club, both of which he had founded. As a member of this group Yeats was introduced to the discussion of the political role of Irish culture. Many of the group associated with Oldham were also associated with Irish nationalism through the Young Ireland Society, which Yeats also joined in 1885.

Of these early works Yeats wrote:

I had begun to write poetry in imitation of Shelley and Edmund Spenser, play after play—for my father exalted dramatic poetry above all other kinds—and I invented fantastic and incoherent plots.

The works were in a Romantic mode, the plays set in Arcadian forests and peopled with shepherdesses, goddesses and hunters. This is a kind of writing that had been popular in the Victorian era, and was later dubbed by Yeats 'eloquent and elaborate'. He soon abandoned it in favour of a much simpler style.

Charles Oldham by
John Butler Yeats

WBY

Katharine Tynan

In late June 1885 C.H. Oldham introduced Yeats to the young Irish poet and writer Katharine Tynan. Her book, *Louise de la Vallière and other poems*, had just been published. Tynan was part of a circle of friends and acquaintances centred on the Contemporary Club and the Young Ireland Society, all of whom were interested in Irish culture and nationalism. Yeats became a regular visitor at Whitehall, her Clondalkin home, often staying there on return visits from London in the late 1880s. Yeats's friendship with Katharine Tynan continued until her marriage to Henry Hinkson in London in 1893, though they maintained occasional contact after that. Tynan was an important early influence on Yeats. She publicised his works by reviewing them for newspapers and magazines, a favour he reciprocated.

John O'Leary and Young Ireland

In 1885 John O'Leary, a leader of the Fenians, returned to Ireland from Paris. O'Leary's house soon became focal point for anyone who was interested in Irish culture and nationalism, and there Yeats regularly met and talked with many of his contemporaries, including Katharine Tynan, Rose Kavanagh, George Sigerson, J.F. Taylor and Douglas Hyde. Many of these figures also became regulars at C.H. Oldham's Contemporary Club, founded in November 1885. Yeats later wrote:

It was through the old Fenian leader John O'Leary I found my theme . . . His long imprisonment, his longer banishment, his magnificent head, his scholarship, his pride, his integrity, all that aristocratic dream nourished amid little shops and little farms, had drawn around him a group of young men.

Another visitor around this time was Maud Gonne—who claimed to remember meeting Yeats at John O'Leary's house, though Yeats dates their first meeting to 1889.

Katharine Tynan's house
at Clondalkin

Katharine Tynan.
Portrait by John
Butler Yeats

John O'Leary (opposite)

A FLOWER HAS BLOSSOMED

Under John O'Leary's influence, Yeats joined the Young Ireland Society in October 1885. It may be that in 1886 he took the Fenian oath, a much more radical political step, but there is no evidence of this. Yeats shared many interests in common with other Young Irelanders, particularly the ambition to develop an Irish national literature. He contributed his poem 'King Goll' to a volume entitled *Poems and ballads of Young Ireland*, published in 1888. Many of the contributors to this volume were friends he had met at John O'Leary's house.

1886

Mohini Chatterjee

Mohini Chatterjee visited Dublin in April 1886 as a representative of the Theosophical Society. Chatterjee was a Bengali Brahmin and an early member of the Theosophical Society of India. He provided translations of Indian works to Helena Blavatsky. Yeats hosted Chatterjee on his visit to Dublin and was very impressed by him. In a letter to Sarah Purser, Charles Oldham described Chatterjee thus:

very like the pictures one sees of Christ. Very gentle. Talks, talks, talks: much like a stream on hillside under grass:—you listen tho' you don't understand—yet it is pleasant afterwards to remember that you did listen awhile . . .

Yeats used Chatterjee's tenets in the poem 'Kanva on himself', and other poems of the period display Indian themes, such as 'The Indian upon God' and 'Anashuya and Vijaya'. The poem 'Mohini Chatterjee', written early in 1929, is a radical simplification and reworking of 'Kanva on himself'. The Dublin Hermetic Society changed its name to the Dublin Theosophical Society on the occasion of Chatterjee's visit in April 1886. However, Yeats and George Russell remained outside it, both being more interested in the hermetic traditions—that is, the largely neo-Platonic and magical doctrines attributed to Hermes Trismegistus and reputedly derived from the wisdom of ancient Egypt.

Douglas Hyde

Mohini Chatterjee

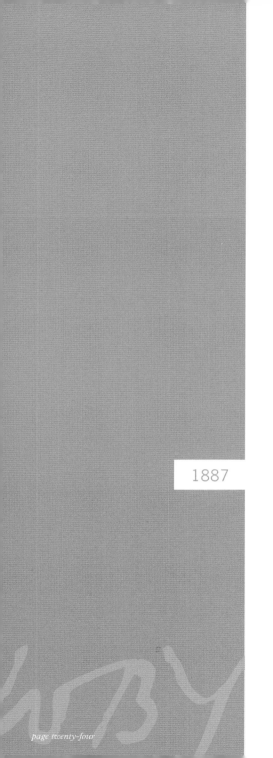

A FLOWER HAS BLOSSOMED

'Mosada'

In June 1886 Yeats's dramatic poem 'Mosada' appeared in the *Dublin University Review*. Encouraged by his father and with assistance from Edward Dowden, Yeats had the poem printed as a 12-page booklet that was published in October 1886, becoming in effect his first book. Instead of providing an illustration of a scene from the poem for the frontispiece, John Butler Yeats provided a portrait sketch of Yeats. His father also helped raise subscriptions to pay for the printing, and pressed the book on visitors to his studio. These visitors included Gerard Manley Hopkins, who wrote of John Butler Yeats's portrait that 'For a young man's pamphlet this was something too much, but you will understand a father's feeling.' Yeats included 'Mosada' in his collection *The wanderings of Oisin and other poems*, but dropped it from *Poems* (1895) and subsequent collections.

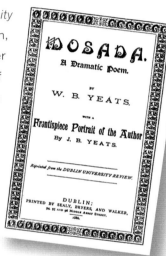

1887

Writing in Sligo

In August 1887 Yeats travelled to Rosses Point in Sligo, where he stayed with his uncle George Pollexfen. During his stay he worked on his long dramatic poem, 'The wanderings of Oisin' and collected fairy and folk tales. Ernest Rhys had already suggested the possibility of Yeats editing Irish volumes for Scott's *Camelot* series of books, and in February 1888 commissioned a collection, which was later published as *Fairy and folk tales of the Irish peasantry*. In October Yeats stayed with his grandparents in Sligo, and he finished 'The wanderings of Oisin' there in November. Later that month he stayed with Katharine Tynan in Dublin. John O'Leary started organising subscriptions for the publication of *The wanderings of Oisin and other poems*.

October
1886

W B Yeats
10 Ashfield Terrace

Harold's Cross

Dublin

1.

Oisin and the Islands of Youth.

Patrick

Oisin tell me the famous story
Why thou out liveth old and hoary
The bad old days thou were't & men sing
Trapped of an amorous demon thing

Oisin

'Tis sad remembering in old years
The swift innumerable spears
The long haired warriors and the feast
And low in the hours when youth has ceased
Yet will I make all plain for thee
We rode in sorrow with strong hounds three
Bran sgeolan and Lomair
On a misty morning mild and fair
The mist drops drops hung on the fragrant tree
And in the blossoms hung the bees
We rode in sadness down lough la lough Lein
For our best were dead on Gabhra plain

Manuscript of 'The
wanderings of Oisin'

George Pollexfen

1888

G.B. Shaw

On 12 February 1888 Yeats met George Bernard Shaw for the first time at William Morris's house. They met there again in April at a lecture on anarchism, and these meetings proved the beginning of a long relationship between the two writers. At the time Shaw was in a relationship with the actress Florence Farr with whom Yeats also became involved. In response to Farr's request for plays from them, Yeats wrote *The land of heart's desire*, and Shaw wrote *Arms and the man*, both performed at the Avenue Theatre in 1894. In 1900 Yeats asked Shaw to write a play for the Irish Literary Theatre and in September 1904 Shaw sent him *John Bull's other island*. In 1909 the Abbey produced Shaw's *The shewing up of Blanco Posnet* in defiance of Dublin Castle, after the play had been banned in England. Yeats also ensured Shaw's election to the Academic Committee of the Royal Literary Society in 1911, and Shaw was instrumental in planning and organising the Irish Academy of Letters in 1932. Shaw was awarded the Nobel Prize for Literature in 1925, two years after Yeats received it.

Bedford Park

In March 1888 John Butler Yeats moved the family to a pleasant house at 3 Blenheim Road, Bedford Park. Designed by architect Richard Norman Shaw, Bedford Park was the first garden suburb in the UK, with houses placed on tree-lined streets, and railway access to the city. Norman Shaw even designed a pub, the Tabard Inn, named after the inn from which Chaucer's pilgrims set off for Canterbury, where Yeats occasionally had a drink. Bedford Park was designed using many of the principles of the Arts and Crafts Movement, and not surprisingly many artists and writers came to live there. Contacts made through other Bedford Park residents helped the young Yeats to extend his London network. The Yeatses became friendly with the family of William Morris, and Lily started work for May

The Priest of Coloony

Good Father John O'Hart
In Penal Days rode out
To a Shanneen in his freelands
With his snipe-marsh and his trout.

In trust took he John's lands
— Sleiveens were all his race —
He gave them as dowers to his daughters
And they married beyond their place.

But Father John went up
And Father John went down
And he wore small holes in his shoes
And he wore large holes in his gown.

All loved him only the shanneens,
Whom the devils have by the hair,
From their wives and their cats and their children
To the birds in the white of the air.

The birds for he opened their cages
As he went up and down
And he said with a smile have peace now
And he went on his way with a frown.

But if when any one died
Came keeners hoarser than the rooks
He bade them give over their keening
For he was a man of books.

These were the works of John
When weeping score by score
People came into Coloony
For he'd died at ninty four

Then was not human keening
The birds from Knocknarea
And the world near Knocknashee
Came keening in that day.

Keening from Innismurry
Nor stayed for bit and sup
This way were all reproved
Who dig old customs up

WB Yeats

Ye PLEIADES
A Monthly Magazine
EDITED BY
EC Yeats
Number 3
Vol 1

Home-made magazine
from Bedford Park

George Bernard Shaw

Bedford Park
(opposite)

A FLOWER HAS BLOSSOMED

Morris as an embroiderer. Their immediate next-door neighbour from 1893 was the publisher Elkin Mathews, who published some of Yeats's early books, and Edwin Ellis, who worked with Yeats on an edition of William Blake's works, also lived at Bedford Park. The Bedford Park Club was a centre for drama, lectures and debate frequently attended by the Yeatses. In May 1889 Jack helped Yeats paint the ceiling of his bedroom and in November persuaded him to shave off his beard ('the symbol I knew myself by', as Yeats referred to it). At home, all of the siblings collaborated in the production of a magazine, *Ye Pleiades*. Bedford Park remained the Yeats family home until 1902, and they were happy there.

Ye Pleiades →

THE SECRET ROSE

Had I the heavens' embroidered cloths,

Enwrought with golden and silver light,

The blue and the dim and the dark cloths

Of night and light and the half-light,

I would spread the cloths under your feet:

But I, being poor, have only my dreams;

I have spread my dreams under your feet;

Tread softly because you tread on my dreams

HE WISHES FOR THE
CLOTHS OF HEAVEN

'The wanderings of Oisin'

The year 1888 had proved very successful for Yeats. He met W.E. Henley, editor of the *Scots Observer* (later the *National Observer*) where many of Yeats's poems and articles were to appear. He made contact with a number of significant figures in London's literary circles and had started giving lectures at the Southwark Irish Literary Club. Christmas Day 1888 was spent with Oscar Wilde and his family at their beautiful house on Tite Street where Oscar read him the proofs of 'The decay of lying'.

1889 was also to be a momentous year. In January his first major book, *The wanderings of Oisin and other poems*, was published by Kegan Paul. Yeats and his friends had spent most of 1888 finding subscribers to make the publication economically viable. The book contained not only the new poem 'The wanderings of Oisin', but also several poems that had appeared in print in various magazines and newspapers, such as 'The stolen child'. Reviews by friends of his in Dublin and London were among the many, mostly favourable, that the book received.

'The wanderings of Oisin' as well as 'The stolen child' reflect the transition Yeats was making at this time, from his youthful Romantic phase to a style which was simpler, more emotional and more Irish. His first major book marks the emergence of Yeats the lyrical Celticist, and the beginnings of the type of poetry he was to develop and perfect during the first half of his life.

WBY as 'King Goll' by
John Butler Yeats

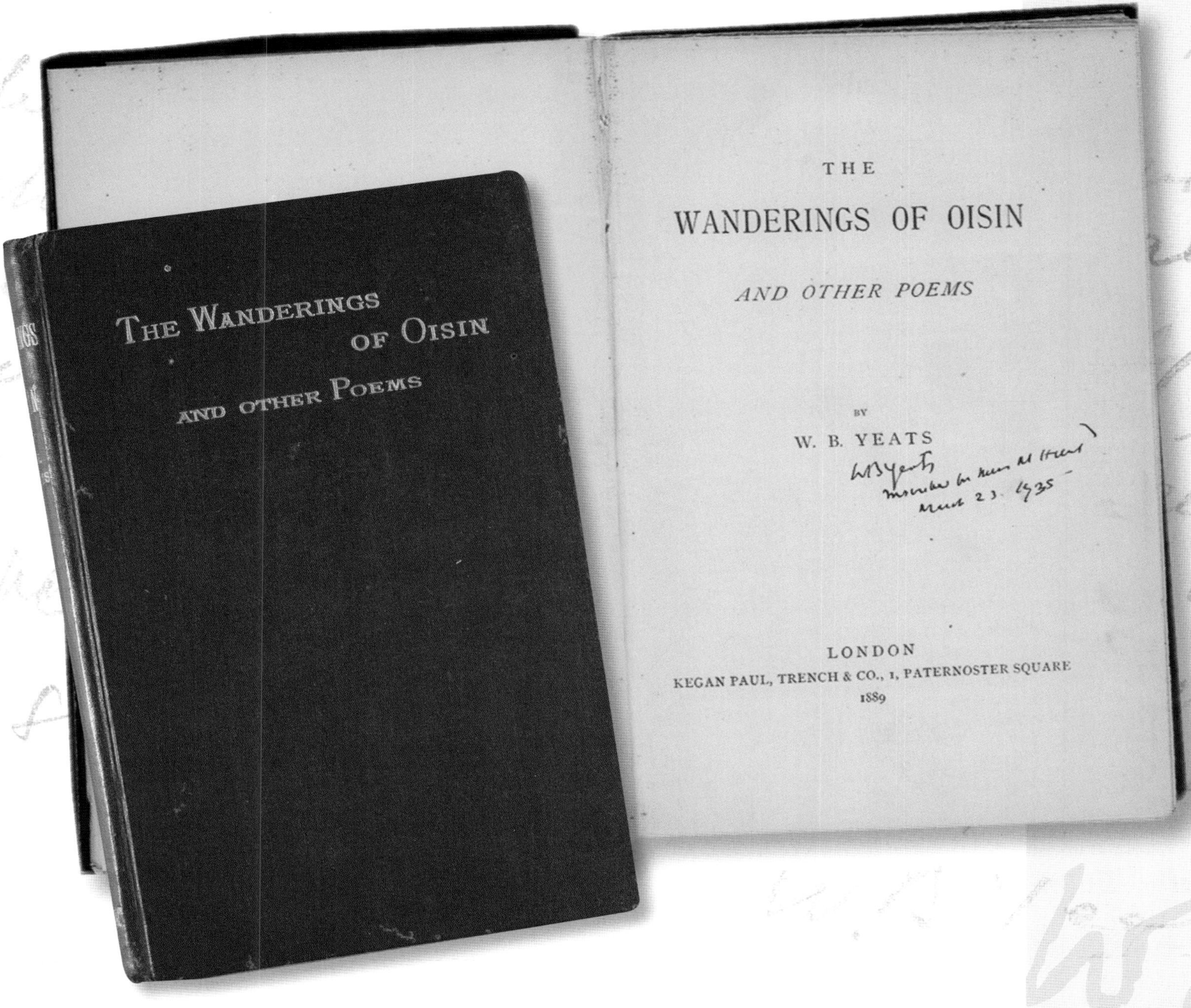

The Wanderings of Oisin and other Poems
THE
WANDERINGS OF OISIN
AND OTHER POEMS
BY
W. B. YEATS
LONDON
KEGAN PAUL, TRENCH & CO., 1, PATERNOSTER SQUARE
1889

Maud Gonne

January 1889 was a significant month in Yeats's life for another reason. On the thirtieth of the month he met the 22-year-old Maud Gonne for the first time when she arrived at the Yeats family home at Blenheim Road to visit John Butler Yeats. As Yeats recorded later, with this visit 'the troubling of my life began'. Certainly she made an impression. Yeats's sisters noticed that she was wearing slippers, but the fact that she kept the hansom cab waiting outside during her visit was an extravagance that could not fail to impress the cash-strapped Yeats family. Gonne told Yeats that she had cried when she read *The island of statues* and that she liked the character of the enchantress, the character modelled on Laura Armstrong. In his *Memoirs* Yeats wrote of her, 'I had never thought to see in a living woman so great beauty. It belonged to famous pictures, to poetry, to some legendary past.'

Maud Gonne was born in 1866 to Thomas Gonne, a captain in the British Army, and his wife Emma (*née* Cook). Her mother died in 1871 when Maud was just five years old and both she and her sister Kathleen were sent to London to live with their mother's aunt Augusta and later Augusta's brother Sir Francis Cook. Maud spent much of her childhood and early adulthood travelling around Europe as companion to her father. The death of Thomas Gonne in 1886 left Maud and her sister independently wealthy. While in France, Maud met Lucien Millevoye, a lawyer and political journalist, and in 1888 they became lovers. She later returned to Ireland and met Michael Davitt, C.H. Oldham and John O'Leary, and began agitating for tenants' rights and revolution.

Maud Gonne in her
apartment on the
Avenue d'Eylau in
Paris, *c.* 1890

Studio portraits of
Maud Gonne

WBY as a young man

page thirty-three

Rhymers' Club

On 11 January 1890 Yeats and Ernest Rhys founded the Rhymers' Club, a forum for contemporary poets. The Rhymers met at the Cheshire Cheese pub in Fleet Street and the group included poets such as Ernest Dowson, Edward Garnett, Lionel Johnson, Arthur Symons, and Richard La Gallienne. They provided each other with mutual support, publishing the short-lived *Weekly Review* to which Rhymers contributed, and two collections of poetry, *The book of the Rhymers' Club* (1892) and *The second book of the Rhymers' Club* (1894). Their bohemian decadence was enhanced by the presence of John Gray and the painters Charles Ricketts and Charles Shannon.

Golden Dawn

In his search for knowledge of the occult, Yeats had joined the esoteric section of the Theosophical Society in 1888, and had been elected to its Occult Research Committee in December 1889. In October 1890, however, Yeats was asked to resign over an article about the Society's *Lucifer* magazine that appeared in Symons's *Weekly Review*. By this time he had found another focus for his interests in the Hermetic Order of the Golden Dawn. He had been initiated into the Order on March 7 by Mina Bergson, sister of the Nobel Prize-winning philosopher Henri Bergson, and later wife of MacGregor Mathers.

Arthur Symons

Cheshire Cheese pub

MacGregor Mathers
(opposite)

WBY

Florence Farr

Yeats first encountered Florence Farr when she acted in a production of a play by John Todhunter, *A Sicilian idyll*, performed in the Bedford Park Playhouse on 5 May 1890. He was fascinated by her and gave the play a rave review. Although at that time she was embarking on an affair with George Bernard Shaw, she and Yeats established a friendship which flourished over many years. Over the next decade Farr cooperated with Yeats on several dramatic ventures, most notably producing and acting in his play *The land of heart's desire* in the Avenue Theatre and experimenting with verse-speaking using the psaltery.

'The lake isle of Innisfree'

On 13 December 1890 Yeats's poem 'The lake isle of Innisfree' was published in the *National Observer*. It became one of his best known and most popular works, a fact that caused him some embarrassment in later life. Its popularity endures: in a survey designed to select Ireland's 100 most popular poems conducted by the *Irish Times* in 1999, it was voted number one.

1891

Rejection

On 3 August 1891 Maud Gonne told Yeats 'of a dream of some past life. She and I had been brother and sister somewhere on the edge of the Arabian desert, and sold together into slavery.' This seemed to confirm such a close spiritual association between them that Yeats proposed to her straight away. Maud Gonne, however, refused his proposal and indicated that they could only be friends. The following day they visited Howth together, after which he wrote 'The white birds'—since she had told him that if she could be any bird she would be a seagull. During August 1891, he wrote a series of poems for her including 'He wishes for the cloths of heaven' and 'He tells of the perfect beauty'. Later in August, Maud Gonne returned to Paris where her son by Lucien Millevoye, Georges, was seriously ill. Yeats was not aware until much later that the child was Maud Gonne's own, believing the story that she had adopted him.

THE LAKE ISLE OF INNISFREE

I will arise and go now, and go to Innisfree,
And a small cabin build there, of clay and wattles made ;
Nine bean rows will I have there, a hive for the honey bee,
And live alone in the bee-loud glade.

And I shall have some peace there, for peace comes dropping slow,
Dropping from the veils of the morning to where the cricket sings;
There midnight's all a glimmer, and noon a purple glow,
And evening full of the linnet's wings

I will arise and go now, for always night and day
I hear lake water lapping with low sounds by the shore;
While I stand on the roadway, or on the pavements gray,
I hear it in the deep heart's core.

W·B·Yeats

Printed and Published by Elizabeth·C·Yeats at the Cuala Press.

Florence Farr
(and opposite)

'The lake isle of
Innisfree' (Cuala
Press)

WBY reading

Parnell's death

On 6 October 1891 Charles Stewart Parnell, leader of the Irish Party at Westminster, died in Brighton. His death, following quickly from his fall from power and the political division of the country, made a marked impression on Yeats, and Parnell became a significant symbolic figure in his poetry. Yeats stated afterwards that following Parnell's death 'the romance of Irish public life had gone and that the young, perhaps for many years to come, would seek some non-political form for national feeling'. This form, Yeats hoped, would be the cultural nationalism in which he was involved. His elegy on Parnell's death, 'Mourn—and then onward!', was published in *United Ireland* on 10 October 1891.

Late that same night, Yeats was at the docks to meet the boat that not only carried Parnell's body back to Ireland but also brought Maud Gonne. She was dressed in mourning, which Yeats assumed was for Parnell—but which was actually for Georges, her son, about whose parentage Yeats and most people were entirely ignorant, and who had died at the end of August, aged two. She was still deeply distressed and wanted to find out if the child could be reincarnated. To this end she attended séances with Yeats and George Russell during her stay, and Russell assured her that the child could indeed be reborn. Around this time Yeats wrote the poem 'Cycles ago', about Maud Gonne's dream in August 1891 about them being brother and sister in a previous life. 'When you are old', based on Ronsard's 'Quand vous serez bien vielle', which was destined to become another of Yeats's most popular poems, was also written at this time. Before Gonne left Dublin, he presented her with a vellum notebook containing several poems and entitled *The flame of the spirit*. Early in November she was initiated into the Golden Dawn in London on her way back to Paris, where she was reunited with her lover Lucien Millevoye. In December 1893 she conceived a second child with him at the tomb of their dead child Georges. This child, a daughter, was born on 6 August 1894 and named Iseult.

Special Extra Supplement, gratis with the WEEKLY FREEMAN, October 10th 1891.

CHARLES STEWART PARNELL,

DIED OCTOBER 6th 1891

See page 4.

Poetry.

MOURN—AND THEN ONWARD!

Ye on the broad high mountains of old Eri,
  Mourn all the night and day,
The man is gone who guided ye, unweary,
  Through the long bitter way.

Ye by the waves that close in our sad nation,
  Be full of sudden fears,
The man is gone who from his lonely station
  Has moulded the hard years.

Mourn ye on grass-green plains of Eri fated,
  For closed in darkness now
Is he who laboured on, derided, hated,
  And made the tyrant bow.

Mourn—and then onward, there is no returning
  He guides ye from the tomb ;
His memory now is a tall pillar, burning
  Before us in the gloom !

W. B. YEATS.

'Mourn—and then onward!', written on the death of Parnell, 1891

page thirty-nine

1892

Irish Literary Society

The Yeats house at Blenheim Road became a centre for expatriate Irish cultural and political discussion, and it was there at the end of December 1891 at a meeting attended by D.J. O'Donoghue, T.W. Rolleston and John Todhunter, that the establishment of an Irish Literary Society in London was mooted. In January 1892 he attended a meeting at the Clapham Reform Club at which the Society was formally established. Days later, Yeats gave a lecture to the Clapham branch of the Irish League entitled 'Nationality and literature', and a first meeting of the Irish Literary Society was held on 13 February. By May, the idea for an Irish National Literary Society, based in Dublin, had developed and a provisional committee was set up. In July Yeats met with Sir Charles Gavan Duffy to discuss a national publishing company, an idea that Duffy and T.W. Rolleston appropriated, much to Yeats's dismay.

The Countess Cathleen

The Countess Cathleen was a play written for Maud Gonne. Its immediate source was a story about a countess who sells her soul to the devil in order to obtain money for her starving tenants—a story which Yeats described as a west of Ireland folk tale, but which in fact was a literary story by a French writer, Leo Lespés. The character of the Countess in the play—a beautiful, noble, self-sacrificing heroine, with a radical political viewpoint—was modelled on Maud Gonne. The work gave Yeats much trouble and became the most often revised of his 26 plays.

A reading of *The Countess Kathleen* took place at the Atheneum Theatre, London, in 1892, although the first major production of the play would have to wait until 1899, when a revised version was performed on the opening night of the Irish Literary Theatre.

The play formed a major part of Yeats's second collection, *The Countess Kathleen and various legends and lyrics*, published by Unwin in mid-August 1892.

The Countess Cathleen

By W. B. YEATS

Volume I. of Dublin Plays

PRICE ONE SHILLING NET

WBY with John
Todhunter, *c.* 1890

Irish Literary Theatre,
1899.

"THE COUNTESS CATHLEEN"
By W. B. YEATS,

AND

"THE HEATHER FIELD"
By EDWARD MARTYN,
Will be performed for the first time in
THE ANTIENT CONCERT ROOMS.

The Countess Cathleen, *May 8th, 12th, 13th, and*
Matinee May 10th.
The Heather Field, *May 9th, 10th & Matinee May 13th*

BY A

Specially-selected Company of Professional Artistes
Under the General Management of
MISS FLORENCE FARR

STAGE MANAGER - - - - Mr BEN WEBSTER

MUSIC CONDUCTED BY HERR BAST & Mr. P. DELANY.

Scenery and Hall arrangements by Mr. BRENDAN STEWERT.
Costumes by NATHAN, and CLARKSON, of London.

PRICES

Reserved & Numbered Seats, 4s.; Area, 2s. 6d.; Balcony, 1s.
Plan and Booking at Messrs. PIGOTT'S, Grafton St.

Corrigan & Wilson, Printers, 24 Upr. Sackville St.

Douglas Hyde

Yeats had been introduced to Douglas Hyde by C.H. Oldham in 1885, and their paths had crossed on a number of subsequent occasions through their involvement with the Irish Literary Society in London and the National Literary Society in Dublin. Hyde's inaugural lecture for the National Literary Society, entitled, 'The necessity of de-anglicising Ireland' was credited with inspiring the foundation of the Gaelic League. However, Hyde's contention that Irish literature could not be written in English rankled with Yeats. Yeats published his response in the *United Irishman* on 17 December 1892, and in May 1893 he gave a paper on nationality and literature in Dublin, based on this article.

1893

Second Order of the Golden Dawn

On 20 January 1893 Yeats underwent the 'portal ritual' for entry into the Second or Inner Order of the Golden Dawn in the Vault of the Adepts at the Golden Dawn temple on Clipstone Street, London. The Outer Order of the Golden Dawn was mainly concerned with teaching initiates the basics of hermeticism. The Second or Inner Order, founded by MacGregor Mathers in 1891, was concerned with practical magic. Yeats took several exams in the subjects he had been studying as a member of the outer circle (for example, alchemical and astrological symbolism, the Hebrew alphabet, the ten Sephiroth and 22 paths of the Cabbalistic Tree of Life, and the tarot trumps). Uniquely, Yeats was not required to wait the symbolic nine months before full initiation as a member of the Inner Order, and the three-part ceremony was carried out immediately after the induction of the portal ritual on 20 and 21 January. During the summer of 1893 he made dozens of visits to the Order's headquarters, attending meetings and perhaps making and consecrating magical instruments. The Inner Order was a secret society; in it, Yeats learned the use of these instruments, as well as talismans, invocation, conjuration and scrying on the astral plane.

LE DIABLE.

L'IMPERATRICE.

LA JUSTICE.

L'ETOILE.

Cartoon by W.T. Horton satirising WBY's involvement with the esoteric

Golden Dawn notebook

Memo.

Robes and Insignia of the Three Adept Officers

Chief Adept. as C.R. — White Robe — Blue Mantle — Blue Sash. Back of Mantle bears an orange coloured emblem of Salt ⊖ 7=4 Breast Jewel — Nemess — Blue and Orange in't. Unaen.

Second Adept — White Robe — Red Mantle bearing green △ emblem on back — Red Sash — Nemess Red & Green — Lamen of Hierophant — Red & Green —

Third Adept — White Robe — Yellow mantle bearing purple emblem ☿ on back — Yellow Sash — Lamen of Hierophant in Orange...

5 □ 6
Adeptus Minor

Three Officers are required
Chief Adept 7=4   Merciful Exempt A   77
Second "   6=5   Mighty A major   7
Third "   5=6   Associate A minor   3T

That is to say these Officers must have attained at least these grades but may be of higher rank and with N or F. The ordinary members of 5=6 are called Very Honoured Frater or Soror. This Grade Consists of 3 Points besides Opening & Closing.

Opening

Members must wear the proper Cloth...

All of this involved a great deal of study and learning. The manuscripts relating to it in the Library's collection reveal the intensity of Yeats's commitment, and the extent of the time and effort he devoted to it. Many of the images and symbols used in the Golden Dawn rituals found their way into his poetry.

The Celtic twilight

In December 1893 *The Celtic twilight* was published by Lawrence and Bullen. The book collected a number of articles, stories and poems that had appeared in Henley's *National Observer* or in other newspapers and magazines since 1888. The articles and stories appearing in *The Celtic twilight* drew on Yeats's work on folk and fairy tales, particularly stories concerned with Sligo and its locality.

The works of William Blake

The works of William Blake, edited by Edwin Ellis and Yeats, was published by Bernard Quaritch in February 1893. In 1900, in his own copy of the book, Yeats wrote:

The writing of this book is mainly Ellis's, the thinking is as much mine as his. The biography is by him. He re-wrote and trebled in size a biography of mine. The greater part of the 'symbolic system' is my writing; the rest of the book was written by Ellis working over short accounts of the books by me, except in the case of the 'literary period' the account of the minor poems, & the account of Blake's art theories which are all his own except in so far as we discussed everything together.

During the course of the research for the edition of Blake, Yeats and Ellis discovered the manuscript of an unpublished text of Blake's *Vala, or the four Zoas*. Yeats also edited a volume of poems by Blake, published by Lawrence and Bullen in 1893. The development of a 'symbolic system' similar to Blake's was something Yeats later pursued in *A vision*.

Drawing of WBY
by Maud Gonne

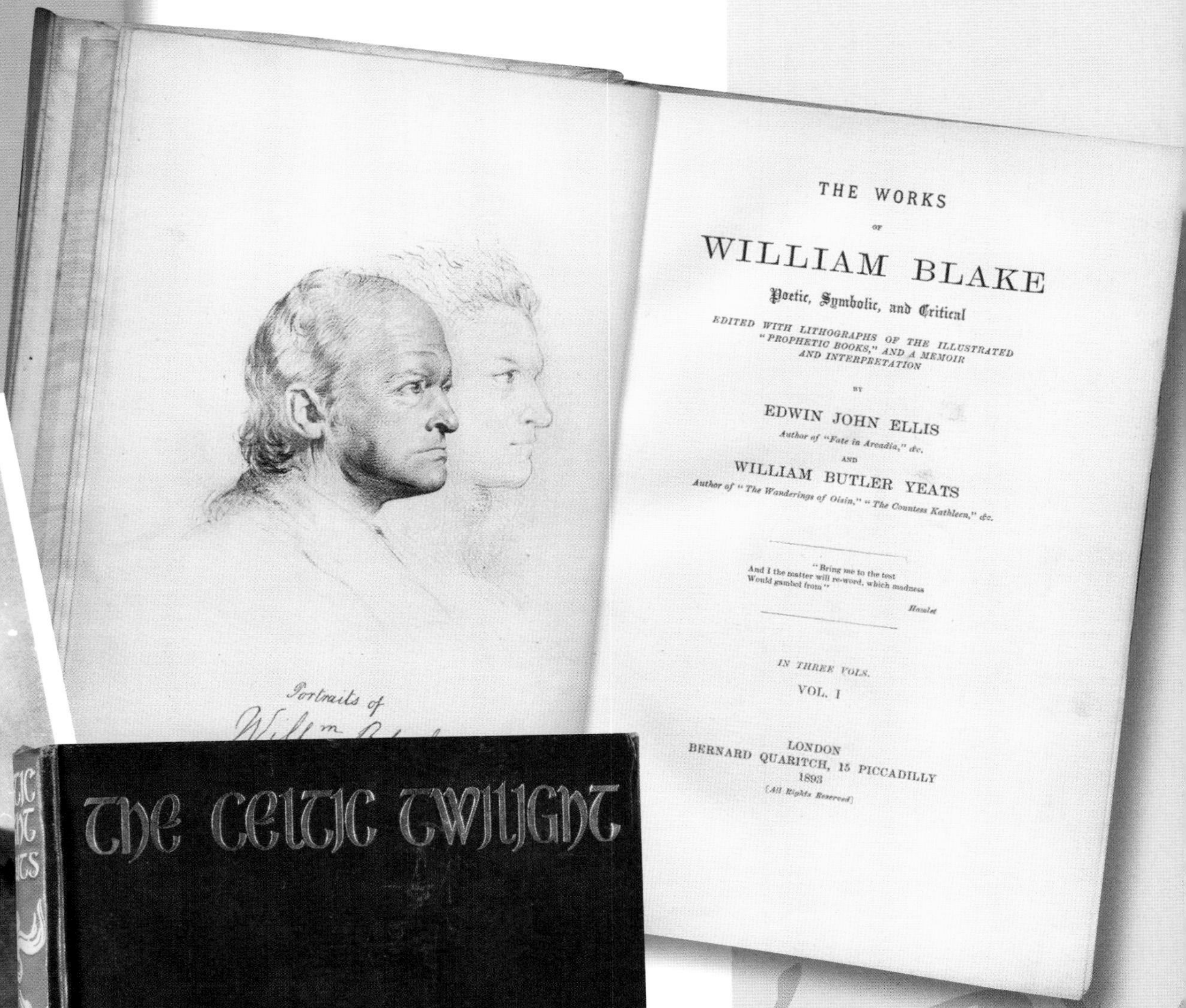

THE WORKS
OF
WILLIAM BLAKE
Poetic, Symbolic, and Critical
EDITED WITH LITHOGRAPHS OF THE ILLUSTRATED
"PROPHETIC BOOKS," AND A MEMOIR
AND INTERPRETATION
BY
EDWIN JOHN ELLIS
Author of "Fate in Arcadia," &c.
AND
WILLIAM BUTLER YEATS
Author of "The Wanderings of Oisin," "The Countess Kathleen," &c.

"Bring me to the test
And I the matter will re-word, which madness
Would gambol from"

Hamlet

IN THREE VOLS.

VOL. I

LONDON
BERNARD QUARITCH, 15 PICCADILLY
1893
[All Rights Reserved]

Portraits of William Blake

W. B. Yeats

THE CELTIC TWILIGHT

1894

Paris

Yeats paid his first visit to Paris during February 1894. At that time Paris was the centre for émigré Irish nationalism (John O'Leary had lived in exile there until 1885), a centre for occult studies, and a major centre of artistic and literary experiment. It was also home to Maud Gonne, and during his visit Yeats saw her several times. She was ill at the time, though Yeats did not realise that she was pregnant. While in Paris Yeats stayed with MacGregor and Moina Mathers (*née* Mina Bergson) and participated in Golden Dawn rituals at their Ahathoor Temple. He also met the French poet Verlaine and called to see Mallarmé, only to discover that he was on a visit to London. On 26 February he and Maud Gonne attended a performance of Villiers de l'Isle-Adam's play *Axël*. This play had a profound effect on Yeats, who started rewriting his own symbolist play *The shadowy waters* on his return to London.

The land of heart's desire

In December 1893 Florence Farr asked Yeats to write a play with a role in it for her niece Dorothy. This became *The land of heart's desire*. Like 'The stolen child', it was based on traditional legends about fairy abductions, and concerned a woman who was taken by the fairies. It was first performed at the Avenue Theatre in March 1894, with Farr in the starring role. It ran in a programme with John Todhunter's play, *The comedy of sighs*, and the poster for the two plays was designed by Aubrey Beardsley. *The land of heart's desire* was revived in April along with Shaw's *Arms and the man,* which had also been written for Farr. Yeats dedicated the play to Florence Farr.

Aubrey Beardsley's poster
for a performance of *The
land of heart's desire*

Scenes from *The land
of heart's desire*

Olivia Shakespear

In April 1894 Yeats met Olivia Shakespear, a cousin of his friend Lionel Johnson. In May she sent him a note via Lionel Johnson to say she would be glad to see him again and by August they were writing regularly to each other. In July 1895 he kissed her on a train journey to Kent. He wrote the poem 'He bids his beloved be at peace' for her, and moved into Woburn Buildings so they could further their affair. She even went shopping with him to find a bed. This was Yeats's first sexual affair, and Olivia Shakespear's first extra-marital affair. The relationship ended in January 1897 and they had little contact again until 1900. From then on, Shakespear became an important focus of his London life and a significant correspondent, though their relationship was never intimate again. He wrote poems about his break-up with her ('The lover mourns for the loss of love', for instance); several poems in *The winding stair* were written for her. In his notebooks he referred to her discreetly as 'Diana Vernon' (the heroine of Walter Scott's *Rob Roy*).

Lady Gregory

On 2 June 1894 Yeats met Augusta, Lady Gregory for the first time, albeit briefly. He visited her with Edward Martyn at Coole Park, her home in Gort, County Galway, in August 1896, and after that he became a regular guest at the house. Coole provided a suitable environment for his writing, and the woods, the lakes and the house itself inspired numerous poems. Lady Gregory became an important collaborator, though Yeats did not always acknowledge the extent of their collaboration. He credited her with co-authorship of *The unicorn from the stars*, and acknowledged her help in rewriting the *Stories of Red Hanrahan* in 1907, though it is now accepted that she also wrote much of *Kathleen ni Houlihan*. He wrote introductions to her books, *Cuchulain of Muirthemne* and *Gods and fighting men*, and addressed his open letter, 'A people's theatre' to her in 1919. Most significant was their work together at the Abbey Theatre. In his *Autobiographies*, Yeats wrote:

WBY's painting (above left) and a photograph (above) of the library at Coole Park

— Olivia Shakespear

— Lady Gregory

THE SECRET ROSE

Lady Gregory, as I first knew her, was a plainly dressed woman of forty-five, without obvious good looks, except the charm that comes from strength, intelligence and kindness.

Lady Gregory was born Isabella Augusta Persse in Roxborough House, near Coole, in 1852. In 1880 she married Sir William Gregory, who was 35 years her senior, and in the following year their only child, Robert, was born. After the death of Sir William in 1892, Lady Gregory began to edit his autobiography, which was published in 1894, and later she published the correspondence of his grandfather, who had served as under-secretary for Ireland between 1812 and 1831. She was religious, with a deep sense of duty and a passionate interest in Irish literature and folklore.

Celtic Mystical Order

During 1895 Yeats set about organising a Celtic Mystical Order. In April 1895 he visited Castle Rock in Lough Key, County Roscommon, with Douglas Hyde, and imagined it as the location for a Castle of the Heroes that would be at the centre of his Celtic Mystical Order. The idea for the Castle of the Heroes had come in part from a novel by Nora Hopper, and Yeats borrowed other ideas from the work of Eugene O'Curry. Colleagues from the Golden Dawn, including his uncle George Pollexfen and the seers Dorothea Hunter and Mary Briggs, helped Yeats explore the supernatural dimensions with a view to instituting forms and symbolism. In December 1897 and during 1898 Yeats continued to develop his ideas, discussing them with Maud Gonne, George Russell and MacGregor Mathers amongst others. His work on the Order brought together his interest in Irish legends and mythology, his interest in the occult and his interest in secret organisations, but much of it may also have been intended to attract Maud Gonne.

WBY's painting of
Coole Park

Lady Gregory

Fountain Court

During September 1895 Yeats moved in with Arthur Symons at Fountain Court in the Temple, just off the Strand; the room was sublet from the psychologist Havelock Ellis. The area around the Temple was popular with literary figures of the day and Yeats was pleased to know that William Blake had also lived there in his old age. Though they had separate rooms at Fountain Court, Symons was not always the most congenial of housemates. On one occasion he borrowed all of Yeats's money, leaving a hungry Yeats to return to his family at Blenheim Road looking for food. Havelock Ellis also provided an unusual influence. Yeats may have read Ellis's essays on Nietzsche, which noted similarities between Nietzsche and Blake, and Ellis experimented with the use of mescal on both Yeats and Symons, using his findings as the basis for an article published in June 1898.

Poems

In October 1895 T. Fisher Unwin published a volume of Yeats's selected works under the title *Poems*.

Unwin had agreed at the end of 1894 to publish a volume, originally to be called *Under the moon*, and in December Yeats started preparing the contents while staying in Sligo. The book contained two plays and a selection of poems originally collected in *The wanderings of Oisin and other poems* and in *The Countess Kathleen and various legends and lyrics*.

Yeats wrote to Unwin in January 1895 stating his concerns about designs for the book ('not green and no shamrocks'). He wrote the preface and made the final revisions in March, and corrected the proofs during June and July. Finally, on 20 August 1895, he received an advance copy of *Poems* at Blenheim Road, and his sister Lily described him with it, saying, 'he can't part from it but sits not reading it but looking at the outside and turning it over and over'. Republished in different editions over the years, *Poems* proved to be a steady seller: Yeats claimed that it sold 20 or 30 times more than all his other books.

Eva and Constance
Gore-Booth (later
Countess Markiewicz),
Yeats stayed at their
home, Lissadell House,
County Sligo, in 1894

Design by H.G. Fell
for *Poems* (1895)

The *Savoy* magazine

The *Savoy* magazine was founded by Arthur Symons and probably named after the London hotel frequented by Oscar Wilde. Yeats was involved with it from its inception and published poems, as well as articles on William Blake, in the eight issues of the magazine that appeared between January and December 1896. Others associated with the magazine were Aubrey Beardsley (the magazine's art editor, whose sister Mabel became a good friend of Yeats), Max Beerbohm, Leonard Smithers (the magazine's publisher) and Olivia Shakespear. Yeats had also been involved with John Lane's publication *The yellow book*, which caused outrage between 1894 and 1897, and there was some concern among Yeats's friends in Ireland that he was becoming too closely identified with decadent artists—a concern that seemed all the more valid after the trial of Oscar Wilde in 1895.

Woburn Buildings

In February 1896 Yeats moved to 18 Woburn Buildings, where he maintained a residence until 1919. Woburn Buildings was located near the British Museum and Euston Station, and was convenient for his trips to Ireland, since the Holyhead train left from there. Ernest Rhys helped him to establish his Monday evenings 'at home' ('Tea & whiskey & no dress', according to Yeats's instructions), and visitors to his rooms included many of the significant figures in literature and the arts of the time. Yeats moved into Woburn Buildings partly to further his relationship with Olivia Shakespear. In his *Autobiographies* Yeats wrote:

On the ground floor at Woburn Buildings lived a shoemaker; on the first floor a workman and his family; I on the second floor; in the attic an old pedlar, who painted a little in water-colours . . . Lady Gregory must have given me the great blue curtain that was a principal feature there for twenty years . . . Presently she gave me the great leather arm-chair which is before my eyes at this moment.

'Some persons of the nineties'.
Cartoon by Max Beerbohm

Woburn Buildings, and
WBY in his salon

Edward Martyn

In the summer of 1896 Yeats stayed at Tillyra Castle, a strange Gothic castle in Galway, the home of Edward Martyn. Martyn, undeniably eccentric, was a Catholic landlord and a talented playwright whose play *The heather field* ran on a double bill with Yeats's *The Countess Cathleen* for the opening night of the Irish Literary Theatre in 1899. Although deeply religious, as well as sharing Yeats's interest in drama and the idea of an Irish national theatre, Martyn was also involved in the occult and they enjoyed Cabbalistic experiments and shared visions during the summer visit, which concluded with a trip to the Aran Islands.

J.M. Synge

On 21 December 1896 Yeats met John Millington Synge for the first time at the Hôtel Corneille in Paris. Shortly afterwards they attended a meeting of Maud Gonne's Paris branch of Young Ireland, L'Association Irlandaise. Synge did not share Yeats's interest in the occult or Irish nationalism, and they were suspicious of each other at first, but Yeats promoted Synge and his work energetically. They met now and then over the next year and during 1898, when Synge spent time on the Aran Islands and visited Yeats at Coole. They remained in close contact as Synge started to write his plays.

Edward Martyn

J.M. Synge. Painting
by John Butler Yeats

1897

The secret rose

On 5 April 1897 *The secret rose* was published by Bullen, with a cover design by Althea Gyles and illustrations by Jack B. Yeats. Yeats dedicated the book to George Russell. The stories collected in *The secret rose* had previously been published in the *Savoy*, the *National Observer* and other magazines and newspapers. In his first years in London Yeats had written numerous articles and stories for a variety of magazines, journals and newspapers to earn money, sometimes writing articles on the same subject for three or more outlets at one time. Only some of this material was collected into volumes like *The secret rose*. Two other stories, 'The tables of the law' and 'The adoration of the Magi', had been rejected by Bullen as being potentially blasphemous and too decadent, but Bullen relented and the two stories were published separately in June.

The secret rose, uniquely among Yeats's work, is essentially a collection of literary short stories, dark in mood and stylistically sophisticated. In this book, Yeats used traditional and mythological sources very much as he used them in his poetry and plays: as inspiration and raw material for literature that was essentially his own creation.

Irish Literary Theatre

As early as January 1897 Yeats discussed with Lady Gregory the idea of establishing what he called a Celtic Theatre. In June the idea was raised again at meetings between Yeats, Lady Gregory and Edward Martyn at Duras, the home of the Comte de Basterot in Galway. The discussions continued during July and August while George Russell was visiting Coole, and Yeats finally drafted a manifesto for a Celtic Theatre. In October the name was changed from the Celtic Theatre to the Irish Literary Theatre, and during November Yeats and Martyn continued to press ahead with their plans, looking for suitable venues for drama presentations and discussing the issue of a patent for the new theatre. The Irish Literary Theatre held its first season in 1899.

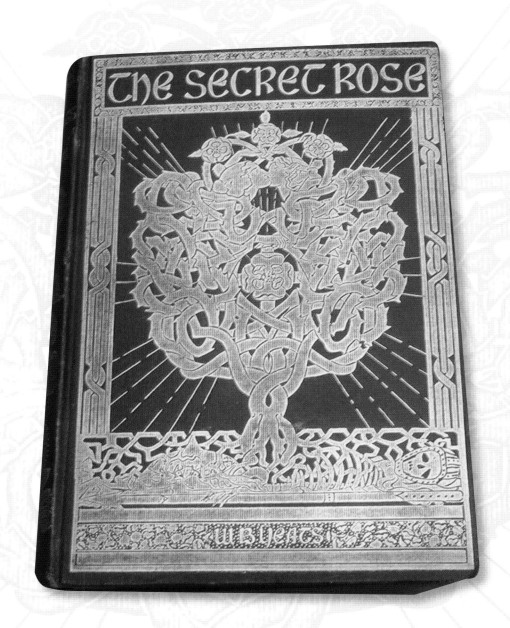

W B YEATS

'98 Committee

In January 1897 Yeats was elected chairman of a London committee established to celebrate the hundredth anniversary of the 1798 Rebellion. The preparations for the commemoration were contentious. Throughout the early months of 1898 Yeats was involved in a hectic round of meetings in connection with the proposed celebrations. Many of these meetings were also attended by Maud Gonne, who had recently returned from America. They both complained about irregularities at the Dublin and London '98 Committees and tensions between the different factions during the year, and they spoke together on a platform in Liverpool in February.

The official celebrations got under way in early August in London and Dublin, with delegates from other countries arriving to represent Irish people abroad. The delegates were met with large crowds wherever they went. The celebrations climaxed on 15 August with a long slow procession from Rutland Square to Saint Stephen's Green, where there was a ceremony to lay the foundation stone for a monument to Wolfe Tone. The ceremony was presided over by John O'Leary and Yeats made a speech, after which they were both guests at a banquet hosted by the Lord Mayor.

A kiss

Not long after the 1798 commemorations, Yeats experienced another momentous event. On 10 December 1898, for the first time in their ten-year relationship, Maud Gonne kissed him on the lips. Sadly, the immediate sequel to the kiss was a confession about her relationship with Millevoye and the parentage of her 'adopted' children. Yeats experienced such emotional turmoil that he claimed he felt 'like a very battered ship with the masts broken off at the stump'. This, however, did not prevent him from proposing once again, on 18 December, nor did it stop her from refusing. She returned to Paris on 19 December, and Yeats spent a miserable December and January wondering whether or not he should follow her. He finally arrived in Paris at the end of January 1899 where at first she refused to meet him. Then, though she told him more about her life, he found her cold and distant. He left Paris in mid-February, suffering from a bad cold.

Companion portraits
of Maud Gonne and
WBY

1899

The Countess Kathleen

On 8 May 1899 *The Countess Kathleen,* the play which had been written for Maud Gonne, had its first performance during the Irish Literary Theatre's first season of plays. Earlier, in January 1899, *tableaux vivants* of the play had been well received by a select audience at the Chief Secretary's Lodge. However, difficulties with the play started during rehearsals in March, when Edward Martyn threatened to resign due to objections he had to its theological and ethical attitudes. Yeats canvassed a Jesuit priest who passed the play with only minor changes. However, Frank Hugh O'Donnell denounced the play as immoral and anti-Irish in April, and published a pamphlet, *Souls for gold!,* at the end of the month. The production of *The Countess Kathleen* at the Antient Concert Rooms on 8 May inaugurated the Irish Literary Theatre's first season and, apart from a disturbance created by a group of students from the University College, the performance was a success. May Whitty played the role of the Countess, which Yeats had intended for Maud Gonne, who had inspired his creation of the character. Florence Farr played Aleel, the lovelorn bard who was based on Yeats himself. The controversy continued days later when Cardinal Logue denounced the play. Yeats responded to the Cardinal with letters to the newspapers on 13 May.

The wind among the reeds

On 15 April 1899 *The wind among the reeds* was published by Elkin Mathews. Many of the poems came from a notebook Yeats started in August 1893. In June 1896 Elkin Mathews paid him a £4 advance against royalties. On 25 October 1897 Yeats wrote angrily to Mathews from Sligo about the proposed design, saying:

This cover is simply ugly . . . Surely you must see yourself that it is absurd to print a book of verse of any kind of importance with the same kind of common stuff on the cover that you put on a novel.

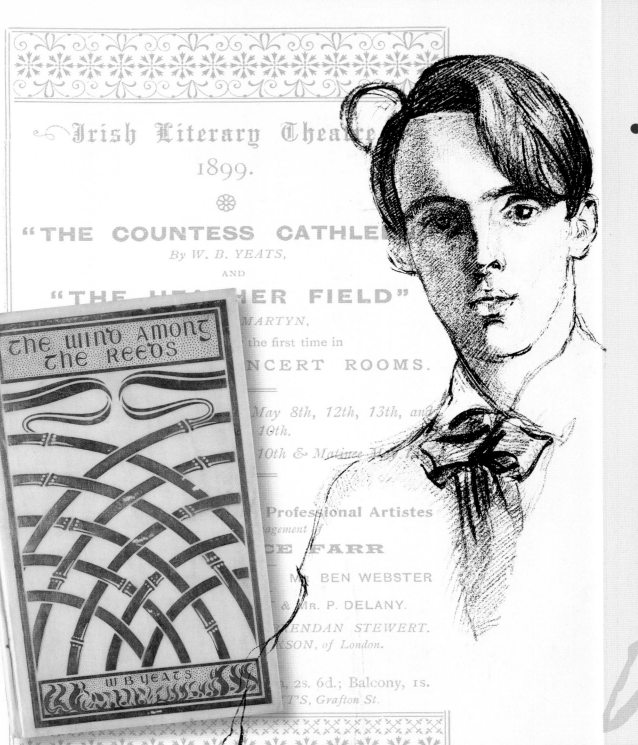

Irish Literary Theatre
1899.
❋

"THE COUNTESS CATHLEEN"

By W. B. YEATS,

AND

"THE HEATHER FIELD"

MARTYN,

the first time in

CONCERT ROOMS.

May 8th, 12th, 13th, and
10th.

10th & Matinee May

Professional Artistes
agement

E FARR

M. BEN WEBSTER

& Mr. P. DELANY.

ENDAN STEWERT.
SON, of London.

2s. 6d.; Balcony, 1s.
T'S, Grafton St.

A portrait of WBY
in his 30s

The wind among the reeds was published while Yeats was rehearsing *The Countess Kathleen* in Dublin. In January 1900 it was voted best book of poems of 1899, for which Yeats received 25 guineas. Around 5 May Unwin published a new selection of his work under the title *Poems*. Having received an advance copy of the book, Yeats wrote to Unwin on 27 April to say that 'the blue cover of my poems is perfect. It is much the best looking book I have ever had.'

The wind among the reeds is a collection of love poems, and includes 'The song of wandering Aengus', 'The fiddler of Dooney' and 'He wishes for the cloths of heaven'. This last poem was first published as 'Aedh wishes for the cloths of heaven' and many other poems were assigned to the characters of Aedh, Michael Robartes, Mongan or Hanrahan.

George Moore

In October 1899 Yeats and George Moore started work on a collaborative project, a play about Diarmuid and Gráinne, based on the well-known medieval Irish romance from the Fenian Cycle. At the same time, Moore was also rewriting Edward Martyn's play *The tale of a town* as *The bending of the bough*, and Yeats took a hand in that too. A year later they met at Coole again and restarted intensive work on *Diarmuid and Grania*—but also started arguing about it, with Moore objecting to Yeats's dictatorial attitude. The situation deteriorated until, in November 1900, Arthur Symons stepped in as adjudicator, although Moore insisted that the terms of their collaboration be written down. A text was finally agreed upon in December 1900, but they continued to make changes and to argue about it early in 1901. The first performance of *Diarmuid and Grania* was at the Gaiety Theatre, Dublin, on 21 October 1901. In July 1902, Yeats and Moore continued their collaboration with a scenario for *Where there is nothing*, which caused greater problems than their collaboration on *Diarmuid and Grania*.

George Moore

THE FASCINATION OF WHAT'S DIFFICULT

I had a thought for no one's but your ears:

That you were beautiful, and that I strove

To love you in the old high way of love;

That it had all seemed happy, and yet we'd grown

As weary-hearted as that hollow moon.

ADAM'S CURSE

1900

Death of Susan Yeats

On 3 January 1900 Yeats's mother Susan died at home at Bedford Park aged 58. She had suffered two strokes in 1887 and had remained withdrawn and depressed until her death from paralysis 13 years later. Yeats wrote to Lady Gregory, saying, 'It has of course been inevitable for a long time; & it is long since my mother has been able to recognize any of us, except with difficulty.' In 1931 he wrote to Lennox Robinson (whose mother had just died), saying, 'My own mother faded out of life while still living and that fading was spread over so many years that there was no moment when we could say "she has gone."' Jack Yeats paid for a memorial for his mother in Saint John's Church, Sligo, where there are also memorials to her parents.

1901

The speckled bird

In June 1901 Yeats visited his family's ancestral home at Sandymount Castle as part of his research for this autobiographical novel. He had started work on the novel early in 1896. It was originally entitled *The benizons of the fixed stars*, then *The lilies of the Lord* and later *The speckled bird* as work progressed slowly and painfully through 1897 and 1898. An advance of £50 ran out but problems persisted. Yeats wrote later:

I had never done a novel of any length & had no knowledge of what I was in for. I went away & wrote till the £50 were exhausted & then I found I was in such a tangle that I had to start afresh.

He restarted the novel but in May 1903 he finally decided to abandon it, and Lawrence and Bullen recouped their £50 advance with *Ideas of good and evil*. The novel charts the spiritual development of Michael Hearne and is centrally concerned with a mystical order similar to the Celtic Mystical Order Yeats was developing at the time. In his *Autobiographies* Yeats refers to *The speckled bird* as 'a novel that I could neither write nor cease to write'. It was not published during his lifetime.

THE SPECKLED BIRD

One evening three boys, the oldest about twelve years old, were in a fort, or "forth" as they would have called it, on a headland on the edge of Galway Bay. About them were some thorn bushes and above them three little oak trees torn and bent by the sea-wind. There was a faint mist on sea and land, and this mist mingling with the paleness and greyness [of] the unmortared stone walls and the heaps of stones in the fields made the world seem fragile, as though it might suddenly dissolve. One of the boys, who was about ten years old and was dressed like a gentleman's son, [was] digging rather wearily, and the other two, who were bare-footed and bare-legged, watched him. Presently he threw down his spade and said, "You are right. It is no use. Yet I am certain that I saw it in my dreams, two or three feet under the grass. I saw a big earthenware pot and it full up of gold pieces."

The oldest boy said, "You only dreamt twice of it, Master Michael. I told you that we should have waited for the third dream. 'They' have taken it away because you did not wait for the third dream."

The younger, who was about eight, said, "I knew that when I said I would not dig any more."

"Well, I am going home," said the boy who had

I

Florence Farr and the psaltery

In December 1901 Florence Farr gave the first public demonstration of speaking verse to the accompaniment of the psaltery. The psaltery, a lute-like stringed instrument, had been developed by Arnold Dolmetsch following discussions with Yeats and Florence Farr. They were interested in the relation between chanting (poetry) and enchanting (magic). Yeats wrote at the time:

Have not poetry and music arisen . . . out of the sounds the enchanters made to help their imagination to enchant, to charm, to bind with a spell themselves and the passers-by?

Yeats gave several lectures on the use of the psaltery and Florence Farr often used it in performances, which were not universally appreciated. 'Cats do the same thing when they are serenading one another,' commented G.B. Shaw after one of Farr's performances. (He had once been her lover.)

On Baile's Strand

In August 1901 Yeats started writing *On Baile's Strand,* his first play about the mythological Irish hero Cuchulain. In a note to the published version, Yeats claimed that much of it had come to him while he was staying at Coole. He was influenced by Lady Gregory's book *Cuchulain of Muirthemne,* published in 1902 with a preface written by Yeats. The tragic heroism of the lonely figure fighting against all odds was particularly attractive to Yeats at the time, and the figure of Cuchulain is an alter ego for Yeats himself, although he later claimed that he had had Parnell in mind when writing *On Baile's Strand.* He completed the play in 1903 and it was first performed at the opening of the Abbey Theatre in December 1904.

Florence Farr with her Dolmetsch Psaltery

◖— Florence Farr and the psaltery

◖ Scenes from *On Baile's Strand*

WBY

1902

John Quinn

In June 1902 Yeats met the American lawyer John Quinn for the first time at the Killeenan Féis. Quinn pressed Nietzsche's work on Yeats, which had an important and lasting influence. With some lapses, they remained friends until Quinn's death in 1924. He often represented Yeats's interests in America, and also successfully defended the Abbey players in Philadelphia in January 1912. Quinn established an Irish Literary Society in New York, with Yeats's old schoolfriend Charles Johnston as president, to promote Yeats and others in America. Quinn also looked after John Butler Yeats in New York, commissioning several paintings from him. He also bought Yeats's manuscripts to raise money for John Butler Yeats's upkeep when the latter lived in New York (a procedure which meant that many of the earlier Yeats manuscripts went to American libraries). In 1922 Yeats dedicated *The trembling of the veil* to Quinn.

Dun Emer Press

In August 1902 Yeats's sisters and father moved from London to Dublin, taking up residence at Gurteen Dhas, a house in Dundrum. His sisters entered into an agreement with Evelyn Gleeson, with whom they established Dun Emer Industries. The company pursued a variety of cottage craft industries along the lines of William Morris's Kelmscott House. Lily was engaged in embroidering, as she had been with May Morris, and Lollie ran Dun Emer Press. Yeats took up the position of literary editor and ensured that Dun Emer Press (and later Cuala Press) published the first editions of many of his books. There were regular quarrels between Yeats and Lollie over editorial and other decisions at the Press, notably in 1906, when it was closed down and replaced by Cuala Press.

GUESTS OF MR. JOHN QUINN
· AT ·
DELMONICO'S · WEDNESDAY · JUNE 24, 1908

John Quinn and guests at
Delmonico's restaurant,
New York, 1908 (above left).
John Quinn and WBY (above)

Dun Emer printing room (far
left) and embroidery room (left)

Kathleen ni Houlihan

The first performance of *Kathleen ni Houlihan* took place on 2 April 1902, with Maud Gonne in the title role. It was produced by William and Frank Fay's Irish National Dramatic Society with Maud Gonne's Inghinidhe na h-Eireann at Saint Teresa's Hall, Clarendon Street. In 1901 Frank Fay had criticised Yeats's plays, claiming that 'They do not inspire; they do not send men away filled with the desire for deeds . . .' With *Kathleen ni Houlihan* Yeats had aimed to write something determinedly nationalistic. Lady Gregory collaborated in writing the play in 1901, and during rehearsals Maud Gonne also pressed Yeats to change the ending and make it more dramatic. The effect of the play certainly was dramatic. One critic later said that 'the effect of *Cathleen ni Houlihan* on me was that I went home asking myself if such plays should be produced unless one was prepared for people to go out to shoot and be shot'. This was reflected in Yeats's poem 'The man and the echo', written in 1938, where he wrote, 'Did that play of mine send out / Certain men the English shot?' Yeats later changed the spelling to *Cathleen ni Houlihan*.

James Joyce

Late in 1902 Yeats met James Joyce for the first time. Yeats later wrote that, at the end of their meeting, Joyce 'got up to go, and, as he was going out, he said, "I am twenty. How old are you?" I told him, but I am afraid I said I was a year younger than I am [Yeats was 37 at the time]. He said with a sigh, "I thought as much. I have met you too late. You are too old."' During November 1902 Yeats introduced Joyce to Lady Gregory and to John Butler Yeats. When Joyce left for Paris later in 1902 Yeats looked after him in London *en route*, and later introduced him to editors in London for whom Joyce might write articles from Paris. Yeats continued to work on Joyce's behalf in London and Dublin, helping to secure grants from the Royal Literary Fund and the Civil List in 1915 and 1916. Though he rejected Joyce's play *Exiles* for the Abbey in 1917, Yeats was impressed with Joyce's writing, claiming in 1923 that Joyce was the only Irishman who had the intensity of a great novelist.

📍 Maud Gonne's entrance in *Kathleen Ni Houlihan,* 1902

● William Fay, actor and co-manager of the National Dramatic Society. Painting by John Butler Yeats

1903

Irish National Theatre Society

On 1 February the Irish National Dramatic Society became the Irish National Theatre Society (INTS), with Yeats as president. It made its London debut in May 1903, and staged controversial performances of Synge's *In the shadow of the glen* later in the year. In 1904 the Society acquired the Mechanics Institute on Abbey Street, which became the Abbey Theatre. The INTS came about as an amalgamation of the Irish National Dramatic Society, which had been founded and managed by the actors William and Frank Fay, and the Irish Literary Theatre. George Russell, who had been involved with both organisations and who drafted the constitution of the INTS, was unanimously elected president of the society but declined in favour of Yeats. Russell, Maud Gonne and Douglas Hyde were elected vice presidents, and William Fay was stage manager. The INTS represented an uneasy alliance, and tension between the Fays and Yeats led to the Fays' resignation in 1908.

Marriage of Maud Gonne and John MacBride

On 21 February, Maud Gonne married Major John MacBride. Yeats had heard of the imminent wedding earlier in the month and had written several letters to Gonne in which he tried to dissuade her from it. One of his main objections was that she was lowering herself by this marriage with 'one of the people', and as a result would lose her capacity to be a respected leader.

In the event, his warnings against the union proved well founded, if for different reasons. A son, Seaghan, later called Seán, was born to the MacBrides in 1904, but a year later the couple parted acrimoniously amid rumours that MacBride perpetrated domestic violence.

Synge controversy

In August 1903 come the first rumblings of trouble over Synge's play *In the shadow of the glen*. Maud Gonne and others protested against its inclusion in the Irish National Theatre Society's season of plays, and in October Yeats wrote a series of articles, published in the *United Irishman*, defending artistic and dramatic freedom in Ireland.

PROGRAMME . . .
IRISH NATIONAL ·
THEATRE SOCIETY,
ABBEY THEATRE. ·

Frank Fay, actor and
co-manager of the
National Dramatic
Society. Painting
by John Butler Yeats

Irish National Theatre
Society programme

THE FASCINATION OF WHAT'S DIFFICULT

In the seven woods

In August 1903 *In the seven woods* was published, the first of Yeats's books produced by his sister Lollie at Dun Emer Press. In a note in the book Yeats claimed to have made many of the poems walking in the seven woods at Coole Park, Lady Gregory's home, before the 'big wind' of 1903 brought destruction and change. His first play about Cuchulain, *On Baile's Strand*, was included in the volume.

American tour

From 4 November 1903 to 16 March 1904 Yeats undertook his first lecture tour in the United States and Canada. He lectured at various venues in New York, Philadelphia, Boston, Saint Louis, Chicago, San Francisco and Washington, as well as Montreal and Toronto. His lectures included, 'The intellectual revival in Ireland', 'Heroic literature of Ireland', 'Poetry in the old time and in the new', 'The theatre and what it might be', and he gave a lecture entitled, 'Emmet, the apostle of Irish liberty' to Clan-na-Gael at the invitation of John Devoy on the centenary of Robert Emmet's execution. In New York he stayed with John Quinn, and on his travels met numerous representatives of the Irish in America and many American celebrities. He dined with President Theodore Roosevelt and his family at the White House on 28 December 1903. Roosevelt was an honorary vice president of the Irish Literary Society of New York, founded by Quinn, and had read works by Yeats and Lady Gregory. Yeats also made arrangements for Macmillan, New York, to become his American publishers.

During his lifetime, Yeats made four more lecture tours in North America, the last in 1932. During a tour in 1920, Mr Junzo Sato presented him with an ancient Japanese sword, which he later wrote about in the poem 'My table'.

IN THE SEVEN WOODS. WILLIAM BUTLER YEATS

WBY, after arrival in the US, 1903

1904

Lane Pictures Exhibition

In November 1904 Hugh Lane, a nephew of Lady Gregory and a renowned art collector, organised an exhibition of contemporary French paintings at the Royal Hibernian Academy in Dublin. He used the exhibition as part of his campaign for the establishment of a gallery of modern art in Dublin. He offered to donate a substantial collection of paintings to such a gallery, and the Dublin Corporation initially agreed to provide a permanent site for the gallery. Other donations for the proposed gallery were given by other public figures, including the Prince of Wales and President Theodore Roosevelt. On 20 January 1908 the Hugh Lane Gallery opened at temporary premises at Clonmell House on Harcourt Street. However, in 1912, arguments with the Corporation led Lane to withdraw certain pictures until a permanent site was provided. In January 1913 the Corporation appealed for assistance for the gallery, but opposition to the plan also grew. Disappointed by the Corporation's lack of enthusiasm, Lane finally withdrew his pictures, lending them to the Tate Gallery in London. Yeats wrote several poems in 1913 concerning the Hugh Lane controversy.

Annie Horniman

Annie Horniman played one of the most crucial roles in the fortunes of the Irish dramatic movement, because it was she who provided the funding for the establishment of the Abbey Theatre in 1904. The heiress to a fortune based on tea, her and Yeats's paths had crossed early in the 1890s, when he had defended her against criticism in the Golden Dawn. She imposed certain conditions on her sponsorship, one of which was that the Theatre would not be narrowly nationalistic in its ideals. Although Yeats remained faithful to the terms of the contract up to a point, Horniman became increasingly critical of the Abbey's nationalistic agenda and eventually transferred her sponsorship to a theatre in Manchester. She was particularly incensed when the Abbey did not close for a night as a mark of respect following the death of Edward VII in May 1910.

mald 1904

WBY, 1904

A proposed design by Edwin Lutyens for the Hugh Lane Gallery, on a bridge across the Liffey

Hugh Lane

The Wo

ekly Social, Political, Literary,

DECEMBER 28, 1909.

WBY

THE FASCINATION OF WHAT'S DIFFICULT

Where there is nothing

Yeats's play *Where there is nothing* had its first performance at the Royal Court Theatre in London in June 1904, followed by a successful run playing to large houses. The play was based on a scenario Yeats had worked on with George Moore in July 1902. Moore, however, had claimed he was using the scenario for a novel and threatened that he would get an injunction against him if Yeats attempted to use it. Yeats went to Coole and used the scenario to write his play in a fortnight in September. Florence Farr conducted a copyright reading of the play in October while John Quinn made arrangements for an American copyright edition, which appeared simultaneously with the publication of the play in the *United Irishman* in November 1902. It caused an immediate rift with Moore, who later refused to speak to Yeats. Yeats later wrote:

I was young, vain, self-righteous, and bent on proving myself a man of action. Where there is Nothing is a bad play . . . I soon came to my senses . . . and in later years with Lady Gregory's help turned it into The Unicorn from the Stars.

The Abbey Theatre

The Abbey Theatre opened on 27 December 1904 in a theatre that had been designed by the architect, diarist and avid theatre-goer Joseph Holloway, in the building formerly housing the Mechanics Institute on Abbey Street. With financial backing from Annie Horniman, a lease on the building had been acquired in April 1904. The first productions were Yeats's *On Baile's Strand* and *Kathleen ni Houlihan*, Lady Gregory's *Spreading the news* and Synge's *In the shadow of the glen*. The opening was a triumph for Yeats, on whom all the limelight was directed, since Lady Gregory was ill with influenza on the opening night. He telegraphed her, saying, 'Your play immense success. All plays successfully packed house.'

The INTS bought the building housing the Abbey Theatre in 1915 for £1,200. It was burnt down in 1951 and the new Abbey Theatre, designed by Michael Scott, opened on the site in 1966.

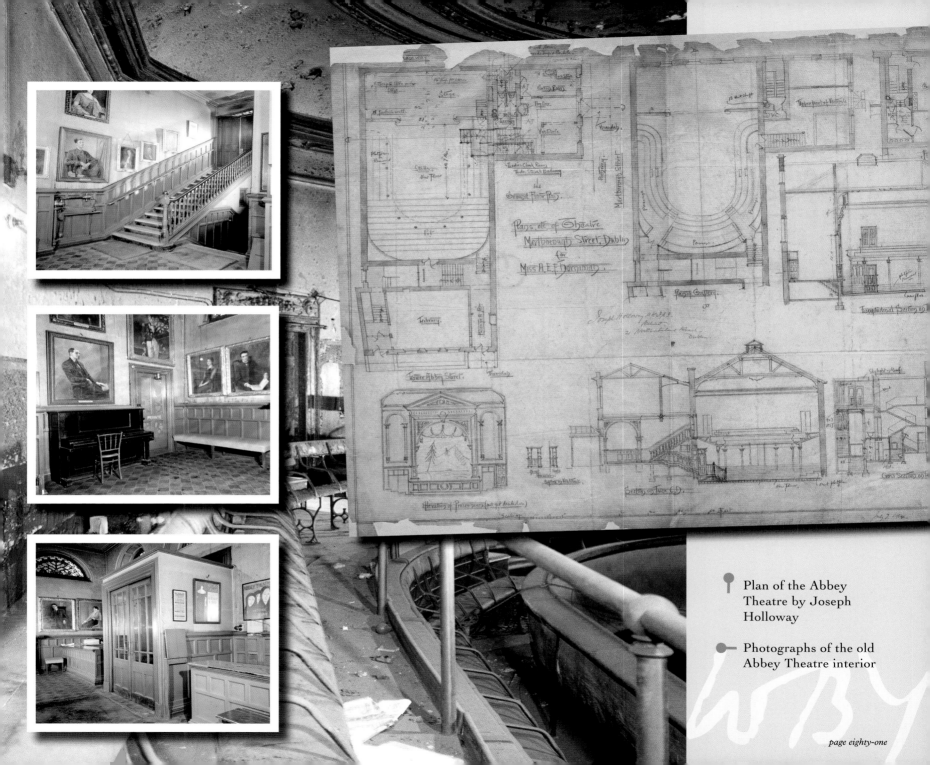

Plan of the Abbey
Theatre by Joseph
Holloway

Photographs of the old
Abbey Theatre interior

1905

The Kelmscott Chaucer

On 13 June 1905, his fortieth birthday, Yeats was presented with a copy of the Kelmscott Chaucer by his friends. The gift had been organised by Lady Gregory and Yeats spent the summer at Coole reading it and sending letters of thanks to his friends. To one friend he wrote, 'It is a book I have longed for some years, indeed ever since it was made. To me it is the most beautiful of all printed books.' The Kelmscott Chaucer was an edition of the works of Geoffrey Chaucer printed by William Morris at the Kelmscott Press in 1896. It was hand-printed on handmade paper, illustrated by Edward Burne-Jones, and issued in a limited edition of 425 copies. Originally sold for £20, it cost Yeats's friends about £40. Yeats treasured his copy, placing it on a blue lectern in Woburn Buildings with two large blue sconces on either side to hold candles.

1907

The *Playboy* riots

On Saturday 26 January 1907 the audience at the Abbey Theatre rioted at the first performance of Synge's play *The playboy of the western world*. Yeats was staying with Professor Herbert Grierson in Aberdeen when he received Lady Gregory's telegram stating, 'Audience broke up in disorder at the word shift.' Yeats was back for the second night on 28 January, and gave a controversial press interview the following day. Irish nationalists, already roused by Synge's stage depiction of Irish peasants, were further incensed when Yeats called the police to the Abbey on Tuesday 29 January and several people were arrested.

HERE BEGINNETH THE TALES OF CANTERBURY AND FIRST THE PROLOGUE THEREOF

The tendre croppes, and the yonge sonne
Hath in the Ram his halfe cours yronne,
And smale foweles maken melodye,
That slepen al the nyght with open eye,
So priketh hem nature in hir corages;
Thanne longen folk to goon on pilgrimages,
And palmeres for to seken straunge strondes,
To ferne halwes, kowthe in sondry londes;
And specially, from every shires ende
Of Engelond, to Caunterbury they wende,
The hooly blisful martir for to seke,
That hem hath holpen whan that they were seeke.

BIFIL that in that seson on a day,
In Southwerk at the Tabard as I lay,
Redy to wenden on my pilgrymage
To Caunterbury with ful devout corage,
At nyght were come into that hostelrye
Wel nyne and twenty in a compaignye,
Of sondry folk, by aventure yfalle
In felaweshipe, and pilgrimes were they alle,
That toward Caunterbury wolden ryde.

THAT Aprille with his shoures soote
The droghte of March hath perced to the roote,
And bathed every veyne in swich licour,
Of which vertu engendred is the flour;
Whan Zephirus eek with his swete breeth
Inspired hath in every holt and heeth

To drawen folk to hevene by fairnesse,
By good ensample, this was his bisynesse.
But it were any persone obstinat,
What so he were, of heigh or lough estat,
Hym wolde he snybben sharply for the nonys;
A bettre preest I trowe that nowher noon ys.
He waited after no pompe and reverence,
Ne maked him a spiced conscience,
But Cristes loore, and his apostles twelve,
He taughte, but first he folwed it hymselve.

The Plowman

WITH hym ther was a Plowman, was his brother,
That hadde ylad of dong ful many a fother,
A trewe swynkere & a good was he,
Lyvynge in pees & parfit charitee.
God loved he best, with al his hoole herte
At alle tymes, thogh him gamed or smerte,
And thanne his neighebore right as himselve.
He wolde thresshe, and therto dyke and delve
For Cristes sake for every povre wight,
Withouten hire, if it lay in his myght.
His tithes payde he ful faire and wel,
Bothe of his propre swynk and his catel.
In a tabard he rood upon a mere.

The Reve
The Millere
The Somnour
The Pardoner
The Maunciple
Geoffrey Chaucer

THER was also a Reve and a Millere,
A Somnour and a Pardoner also,
A Maunciple, and myself; ther were namo.
The Millere was a stout carl for the nones,
Ful byg he was of brawn, and eek of bones,
That proved wel, for over al ther he cam,
At wrastlynge he wolde have alwey the ram.
He was short sholdred, brood, a thikke knarre,
Ther nas no dore that he ne wolde heve of harre,
Or breke it at a rennyng with his heed.
His berd as any sowe or fox was reed,
And therto brood, as though it were a spade.
Upon the cope right of his nose he hade
A werte, and theron stood a toft of herys,
Reed as the brustles of a sowes erys;
His nosethirles blake were and wyde.
A swerd and bokeler bar he by his syde;
His mouth as greet was as a greet forneys.
He was a janglere and a goliardeys,
And that was moost of synne and harlotries.
Wel koude he stelen corn, and tollen thries;
And yet he hadde a thombe of gold, pardee.
A whit cote and a blew hood wered he,

Of maistres hadde he mo tha
That weren of lawe expert an
Of whiche ther weren a dusz
Worthy to been stywardes of
Of any lord that is in Engelo
To maken hym lyve by his pr
In honour dettelees, but if he
Or lyve as scarsly as hym lis
And able for to helpen al a ch
In any caas that myghte falle
And yet this Maunciple sette

THE Reve was a s
His berd was sha
kan;
His heer was by
yshorn,
His tope was do
biforn.

ful longe were his legges and
Ylyk a staf, ther was no calf
Wel koude he kepe a gerner a
Ther was noon auditour kou
Wel wiste he, by the droghte
The yeldynge of his seed and
His lordes sheepe, his neet, hi
His swyn, his hors, his stoor
Was hoolly in this reves gov
And by his covenant yaf the
Syn that his lord was twenty
Ther koude no man brynge h
Ther nas baillif, ne hierde, ne
That he ne knew his sleighte
They were adrad of hym as o
His wonyng was ful faire upo
With grene trees yshadwed
He koude bettre than his lor
ful riche he was astored pryv
His lord wel koude he plesen
To yeve and lene him of his o
And have a thank, and yet a
In youthe he hadde lerned a g
He was a wel good wrighte, a
This Reve sat upon a ful goo
That was al pomely grey, an
A long surcote of pers upon
And by his syde he baar a rus
Of Northfolk was this Reve
Biside a toun men clepen Ba
Tukked he was, as is a frere,
And evere he rood the hyndr

6

TO W.B.YEATS
For June 13. 1905. From
S. C. Cockerell.
Edmund Gosse.
A. H. Bullen.
Wilfrid Scawen Blunt.
A. E. Horniman.
Will Rothenstein.
Augusta Gregory.
Robert Gregory.
E. Montgomery.
Maurice Baring.
Elkin Mathews.
Castletown.
John Masefield.
Arthur Symons.
Charles Ricketts.
C. H. Shannon.
Gilbert Murray.
C. E. Lawrence.
Una Birch.
Hugh P. Lane.
William Orpen.
John Quinn.
A. Sullivan.
R. C. Trevelyan.
Willicent Sutherland.
John Shaw-Taylor.

The Kelmscott Chaucer was given to WBY for his fortieth birthday by his friends

List of subscribers

page eighty-three

Italy with Lady Gregory

Yeats left London on 10 April to join Lady Gregory and her son Robert in Italy. Together they visited Venice, Florence, Rimini, Urbino, San Marino, the Apennines and Ravenna, where Yeats saw the famous mosaics in the cathedral, including those which had been made during the period of Byzantine rule in the late sixth century, possibly by craftsmen from Constantinople. This visit marked the beginning of the poet's love of Byzantine art, which later inspired poems such as 'Sailing to Byzantium' and 'Byzantium'.

In May, while they were staying in Venice, Yeats was summoned back to London when the English Lord Chamberlain (responsible for theatre censorship) threatened to stop a production of *The playboy of the western world*.

Deirdre

In August 1907 Yeats's play *Deirdre* was published by A.H. Bullen. The tragic love story of Deirdre was a popular theme among Irish writers. George Russell had written a Deirdre play and later J.M. Synge wrote one too. Yeats started work on his play in July 1904, but the work was problematic and proceeded only slowly. He continued working on it intermittently through 1904 and 1905 and it was first performed on 23 November 1905 with Letitia Darragh in the title role. Darragh was an unpopular choice and the performances were not well received. Yeats began to revise it immediately and it was performed again in November 1908. The performance of Mrs Patrick Campbell, the leading English actress of the day, earned praise even from Yeats's harshest critics, and audiences cheered performances in London later in the month. Yeats later dedicated the play to her and to the memory of Robert Gregory, who designed the set for her performances. Yeats wrote to John Quinn, saying, 'I am now accepted as a dramatist in Dublin.' A year later Yeats was working on revisions to *Deirdre* again.

YEATS defended The Playboy of the Western World from the stage
of The Abbey. This cartoon is by Tom Lalor.

WBY as defender of
Playboy in a cartoon
by Tom Lalor

Discoveries

On 15 December 1907 *Discoveries,* Yeats's last book under the Dun Emer imprint, was published. He had started writing it in June 1906, and the essays were initially published in the *Gentleman's Magazine* as 'My thoughts and second thoughts'. They show the influence of Nietzsche as Yeats reflects on topics such as his work in the theatre and the development of civilisation.

1908

Love affairs

In March 1908 Yeats began a love affair with Mabel Dickinson. Described as a 'medical gymnast and masseuse', Dickinson had rooms on Nassau Street, Dublin, convenient to the Nassau Hotel, where Yeats stayed on his visits to Dublin, and to the United Arts Club on Lincoln Place where she and Yeats often met and dined. By July 1908 Yeats was doing exercises prescribed by her, and Mabel Dickinson may have been the inspiration for the poem 'The mask', written in 1910. In May 1913 Mabel Dickinson told Yeats that she was pregnant, and he feared that he would have to marry her. The pregnancy turned out to be a false alarm, but the issue brought an end to his affair with her.

During a visit to Paris in June 1908, Yeats spent much of his time with Maud Gonne and her daughter Iseult. In September he experienced mystical unions with Maud Gonne, but when they met again in Dublin in October, he found their relationship restored to its usual unsatisfactory footing. However, on a visit to Paris in December, at the time when he wrote 'No second Troy', they made evocations together and cast horoscopes. It seems that he and Maud Gonne finally became lovers at this time.

Maud Gonne with her children Iseult and Seán, *c.* 1905

WBY

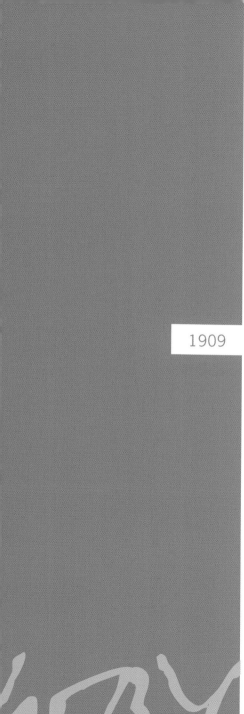

Collected works

Between September and December 1908 eight volumes of Yeats's *Collected works in verse and prose* were published by Shakespeare Head Press, with financial support from Annie Horniman. Earlier in the year, Yeats had quarrelled with A.H. Bullen over the placement of frontispiece portraits in the volumes, but was pleased with the design. At the age of 43 it seemed as if he was summing up his work, but his most significant writing was yet to come.

1909

Death of Synge

On 24 March Synge died of cancer. Yeats wrote, 'Synge is dead. In the early morning he said to the nurse, "It is no use fighting death any longer" and he turned over and died.' Yeats records impressions of the time in a diary, extracts from which were later published as 'The death of Synge'. Yeats, who wished to publish Synge's last works, had several quarrels with Synge's family and lawyers over access to his papers, particularly to the manuscript of *Deirdre of the sorrows*. In July Cuala Press published a volume of Synge's *Poems and translations* with a preface by Yeats. Subsequently, Yeats wrote several essays about Synge, and *Deirdre of the sorrows* was produced at the Abbey in 1910.

Ezra Pound

By the summer of 1909 Ezra Pound, a young American poet, was a frequent visitor at Yeats's Monday evenings 'at home' at Woburn Buildings. Over the following years Pound and Yeats met often, and Pound's criticism of Yeats's poems impressed him. However, they quarrelled when Pound rewrote some poems that Yeats had submitted to Harriet Monroe's magazine, *Poetry*, which was based in Chicago and for which Pound had appointed himself overseas editor. Yeats wrote that Pound had 'a headlong ragged nature, is always hurting peoples feeling [*sic*], but he has I think some genius and great goodwill'. Despite their quarrel, Yeats continued to seek

After the death of Synge (above) Cuala Press (left) published a volume of Synge's *Poems and translations* with a preface by WBY

Pound's advice, and when Harriet Monroe's *Poetry* magazine awarded Yeats a prize for best poem in 1913 (for 'The grey rock'), Yeats asked that most of the money go to Pound. In 1914 Yeats and Pound started a more intensive collaboration when they stayed together in Pound's rented house, Stone Cottage in Sussex.

1910

Gordon Craig

In February 1910 Yeats spent some time working with a model of Gordon Craig's stage screens.

Craig was one of the great innovators in stage design on the twentieth century and his radical ideas about design and lighting appealed to Yeats in his search for a more poetic and less realistic theatre. Yeats saw several productions that used Craig's designs and techniques, and lectured on Craig's innovations during the interval between plays at the Molesworth Hall in Dublin in 1903. Late in 1909 Craig demonstrated his screens to Yeats, and in February 1910 he sent him a model of them. Yeats used the model to try out ideas for staging *On Baile's Strand* and *The land of heart's desire*. The first ever use of Craig's screens was at the Abbey in 1911 for productions of Lady Gregory's *The deliverer* and Yeats's *The hour-glass*.

In October 1910 Yeats's essay 'The tragic theatre' was published in Craig's magazine, the *Mask*, and in 1911 Bullen published Yeats's *Plays for an Irish theatre* with illustrations by Gordon Craig.

CATHAY

TRANSLATIONS BY

EZRA POUND

FOR THE MOST PART FROM THE CHINESE
OF RIHAKU, FROM THE NOTES OF THE
LATE ERNEST FENOLLOSA, AND
THE DECIPHERINGS OF THE
PROFESSORS MORI
AND ARIGA

LONDON
ELKIN MATHEWS, CORK STREET
MCMXV

Ezra Pound (and opposite)

Cathay. Translations by
Ezra Pound

Irish nationalists

In March 1910 Yeats gave a lecture entitled 'The theatre and Ireland' to a Gaelic League meeting attended by Douglas Hyde, Thomas MacDonagh and Patrick Pearse. MacDonagh had dedicated a book of poems to Yeats in 1903, and his play *When the dawn is come* was produced at the Abbey in 1908, when Yeats attended performances with Maud Gonne. MacDonagh was among those who nominated Yeats for the Chair of English at the National University in 1909 (a post he did not get). In 1899 Pearse wrote that Yeats was 'a mere English poet of the third or fourth rank, and as such he is harmless', but in 1908 he wrote that 'it was through [Yeats's] writings that many of us made our first acquaintance with our early traditions and literature. He has never ceased to work for Ireland.' Pearse later claimed that Yeats was 'the poet who has most freely voiced Irish nationalism of our time'.

The green helmet and other poems

In December 1910 *The green helmet and other poems* was published by Cuala Press. It was Yeats's first volume of poetry since the eight volumes of his *Collected works* were published in 1908, and it marked a new departure in his writing. Many of the themes that were to occupy him for the rest of his life are in evidence in this volume, as is the beginning of the harder-edged style of his mature writing. Some of the poems reflect his increasing involvement in and concern with public affairs and the theatre ('The fascination of what's difficult', and 'All things can tempt me'). His identification with the disappearing world of Anglo-Ireland is also apparent in 'Upon a house shaken by the land agitation'. The volume also contains a number of poems inspired by Maud Gonne, including 'A woman Homer sung', 'No second Troy', and 'Reconciliation'. A second edition of the book was published by Macmillan in 1912 containing an additional six poems including 'At the Abbey Theatre'.

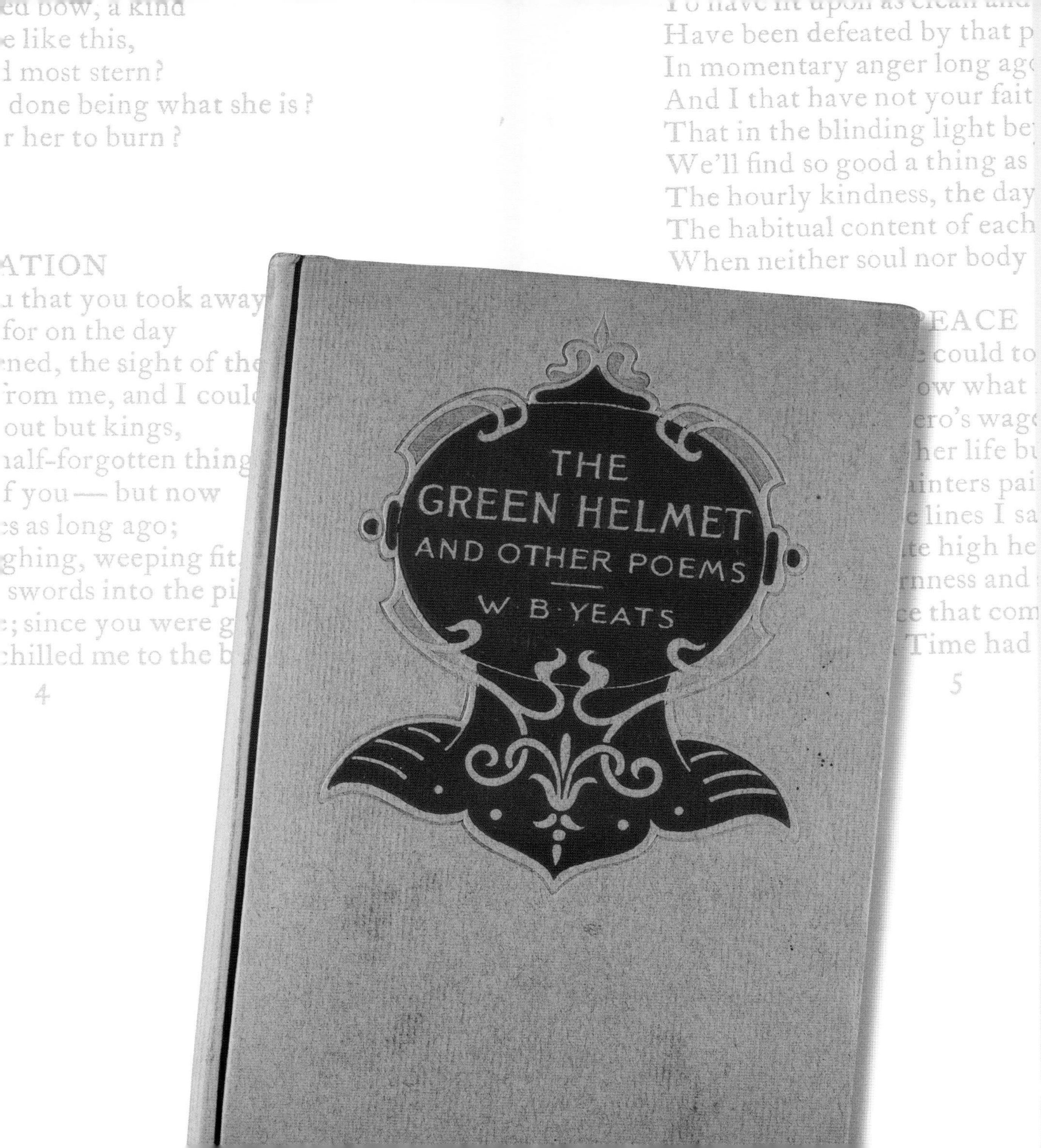

ATION

u that you took away
for on the day
ned, the sight of the
rom me, and I coul
out but kings,
half-forgotten thing
f you — but now
s as long ago;
ghing, weeping fit
swords into the pi
; since you were g
chilled me to the b

4

Have been defeated by that p
In momentary anger long ag
And I that have not your fait
That in the blinding light be
We'll find so good a thing as
The hourly kindness, the day
The habitual content of each
When neither soul nor body

PEACE

e could to
ow what
ero's wage
her life bu
inters pai
lines I sa
te high he
rnness and
ce that com
Time had

5

THE
GREEN HELMET
AND OTHER POEMS
—
W B YEATS

Royal Literary Society and Civil List pension

Yeats was awarded a Civil List pension in August 1910. The pension provided a guaranteed income for life of £150 per annum, and nearly doubled Yeats's income. However, it also gave another weapon to nationalist elements opposed to him. From then on, nationalist commentators referred to him disparagingly as 'Pensioner Yeats', emphasising his persistent relationship with British rule. On the other hand, his pension was threatened after the 1916 Easter Rising, when his loyalty to Britain was questioned.

1912

Leo Africanus

On 9 May 1912, at a séance with American medium Etta Wriedt, Yeats made contact with Leo Africanus for the first time. Other séances in June brought more contact from Leo, and Yeats also heard Maud Gonne's voice. The spirit of Leo Africanus lay behind the essay *Per amica silentia lunae* and also featured prominently in the automatic scripts which George began to write soon after their marriage, and which formed the basis of Yeats's book, *A vision*.

The historical Leo Africanus was a sixteenth-century Arabic writer. He had been born al-Hasan ibn Muhammad al-Wazzan in Spain about 1490, but grew up in Morocco and travelled extensively in North Africa before being captured by the Knights of Rhodes (the Hospitallers, later the Knights of Malta) and given to Pope Leo X. He converted to Christianity, taking the Pope's name, and was generally known as Leo Africanus.

The work for which Leo Africanus is chiefly renowned is *Cosmographia del' Africa*, published posthumously in 1550. He also wrote several other works, mainly on Arabic language and poetics, including an Arabic/Latin/Hebrew dictionary.

American medium,
Etta Wriedt

Rabindranath Tagore and *The post office*

On 27 June 1912 Yeats met the Bengali poet Rabindranath Tagore for the first time. Yeats immediately set about promoting Tagore's work, so successfully that the poet became something of a cult figure. Yeats wrote prefaces and introductions, as well as arranging for the performance of Tagore's play *The post office* at the Abbey and for its publication by Cuala Press. The play was performed at the Abbey on a double bill with Patrick Pearse's *An rí* in 1913, as a fund-raising event for Pearse's school, Scoil Éanna. In December 1912 Tagore was awarded the Nobel Prize for Literature.

Alick Schepeler

During the summer of 1912 Yeats was engaged in an affair with Alick Schepeler. Schepeler was well known in bohemian London circles. She had previously had an affair with Augustus John, and may have been the subject of Pound's poem 'Albâtre'. In September 1912 Yeats was sending her letters full of sexual innuendo from Coole, where he was staying, and in 1914 Schepeler joined him during a stay there. In November 1915, at the same time as he was seeing Alick Schepeler, Yeats was also drafting a series of poems about Maud Gonne.

A letter from Bengali
poet Rabindranath Tagore
(illustrated opposite) to
WBY, 1935

"Uttarayan"
Santiniketan. Bengal

July 16. 1935

Dear Yeats

Your letter seems to come to me from a remote age reminding me of those days of my acquaintance with you intense and intimate. Though I had already left behind me half a century of my life when I visited your country I felt that I had come to the beginning of a fresh existence young with the surprise of an experience in an atmosphere of kindly personalities. I often remember a meeting with you in that chamber of yours, quaintly unique, that seemed to me, I do not know why, resonant of an old world silence, and though I find it difficult distinctly to recollect the subject of our talk the feeling of it lingers in my mind like the aroma of a rich and rare wine.

1913

'To a wealthy man . . .'

On 11 January 1913 Yeats published a poem called 'A gift' in the *Irish Times*. It was later entitled 'To a wealthy man who promised a second subscription to the Dublin Municipal Gallery if it were proved the people wanted pictures'. The wealthy man in question was Lord Ardilaun, an heir to the Guinness fortune. William Martin Murphy, a Dublin newspaper proprietor and transport magnate, took offence at the poem and began attacking Yeats in his newspapers, claiming that he would rather see a 'block of sanitary houses at low rents replacing a reeking slum than all the pictures Corot and Degas ever painted'. Later that year, Murphy's refusal to recognise a trade union was at the centre of the Dublin Strike and Lockout in 1913, and Yeats wrote angrily about the situation in the *Irish Worker* on 1 November 1913. The letter led to a reconciliation between Yeats and George Russell after an estrangement of seven years.

'September 1913'

Originally entitled 'Romance in Ireland (on reading much of the correspondence against the art gallery)', this poem was published in the *Irish Times* on 8 September 1913. It appeared shortly before the Dublin Corporation rejected Hugh Lane's offer of paintings for a gallery of modern art in Dublin. It reflects ideas he had expressed in a *Manchester Guardian* article in July. There, Yeats claimed that 'if the intellectual movement is defeated Ireland will for many years become a little huckstering nation, groping for halfpence in a greasy till'. It was given the title 'September 1913' when it appeared in a slim limited-edition volume entitled *Poems written in discouragement*, published by Cuala in October 1913. This volume also contained 'To a wealthy man . . .', 'To a friend whose work has come to nothing', 'Paudeen' and 'To a shade'.

THE GIFT.

(BY W. B. YEATS.)

[To a friend who promises a bigger subscription than his first to the Dublin Municipal Gallery if the amount collected proves that there is a considerable "popular demand" for the pictures.]

You gave, but will not give again
  Until enough of Paudeen's pence
By Biddy's half-pennies have lain
  To be "some sort of evidence,"
Before you've put your guineas down,
  That things, it were a pride to give,
Are what the blind and ignorant town
  Imagines best to make it thrive.

What cared Duke Ercole, that bid
  His mummers to the market place,
What th' onion sellers thought or did
  So that his Plutarch set the pace
For the Italian comedies?
And Guidobaldo when he made
  That grammar school of courtesies
Where wit and beauty learned their trade,
  Upon Urbino's windy hill,
Had sent no runners to and fro
  That he might learn the shepherd's will;
And when they drove out Cosimo
  Indifferent how the rancour ran,
He gave the hours they had set free
  To Michelozzo's latest plan
For the San Marco Library,
  Whence turbulent Italy should draw
Delight in Art whose end is peace,
  In logic, and in natural law,
  By sucking at the dugs of Greece.

Your open hand but shows our loss
  For he knew better how to live.
Leave Paudeens to their pitch and toss;
  Look up in the sun's eye, and give
What the exultant heart calls good,
  That some new day may breed the best
Because you gave, not what they would,
  But the right twigs for an eagle's nest.

             W. B. YEATS.
January 8th, 1913.

MUNICIPAL ART GALLERY.

FURTHER SUBSCRIPTIONS.

The Municipal Art Gallery Building Fund Committee sat at the Mansion House on Thursday, the 9th inst. Present:—
The Rev. J. P. Mahaffy, C.V.O., in the chair; Hutcheson Poë, Dr. John R. O'Connell, Ser-

---

ngly opposes Mr.
his letter of Satur-
ove obdurate" the
his undoubted right
This proposal, says
ear analysis. It
quarters, and it
in a complete ig-
nstitutional usage.
how the unwisdom
ning silent in face
of Ulster. Plainer
ould not have pro-
f despair. The
admits that his
ional, but he falls
ght of the Sove-
t before the next
ere is no question
there are certain
wn, but they are
In spite of this
policy of the Go-
ssertion after the
however, in our
at the Sovereign
which might lead
between the oc-
majority of his
the possibility,
it to be, of an-
neral Election. A
the exercise of
rio motu regis,
ndication at the
whose advice
roposal, in fact,
its implications
y to be revealed.
Constitution that
advice of his
e, must bear on
responsibility for
heir duty to give
ces on which he
is justified in
Royal assent.
se knowledge
s perhaps un-
h assurances His
solve Parliament

---

the powder magazines. The bodies of the five victims were blown to pieces, to a distance of a hundred yards. A man working on the railway near by was injured by a stone hurled through the air by the force of the explosion.

ROMANCE IN IRELAND.

(On reading much of the correspondence against the Art Gallery.)

What need you, being come to sense,
  But fumble in a greasy till
And add the ha'pence to the pence,
  And prayer to shivering prayer, until
You have dried the marrow from the bone,
  For men were born to pray and save?
Romantic Ireland's dead and gone—
  It's with O'Leary in the grave.

Yet they were of a different kind,
  The names that stilled your childish play;
They have gone about the world like wind.
  But little time had they to pray
For whom the hangman's rope was spun;
  And what, God help us, could they save?
Romantic Ireland's dead and gone—
  It's with O'Leary in the grave.

Was it for this the wild geese spread
  The grey wing upon every tide?
For this that all that blood was shed?
  For this Edward Fitzgerald died?
And Robert Emmet and Wolfe Tone,
  All that delirium of the brave?
Romantic Ireland's dead and gone—
  It's with O'Leary in the grave.

Yet could we turn the years again,
  And call those exiles as they were,
In all their loneliness and pain,
  You'd cry—"Some woman's yellow hair
Has maddened every mother's son"—
  They weighed so lightly what they gave.
But let them be, they're dead and gone:
  They're with O'Leary in the grave.
             W. B. YEATS.
Dublin, September 7th, 1913.

AMERICANS AND THE ART GALLERY.

Letter From Lady Gregory.

TO THE EDITOR OF THE IRISH TIMES.
SIR,—I have not liked to write anything in the controversy as to the site for the Art Gallery, for I thought that was a question for Dublin itself to settle; and, although my husband once represented Dublin in

---

1914

Stone Cottage

From November 1913 to January 1914 Yeats stayed at Stone Cottage in Sussex with Ezra Pound. Yeats wanted to do some concentrated work, and Pound was to act as secretary. They read books on Rosicrucian magic, and Yeats prepared lectures for his forthcoming American lecture tour. Most importantly, Yeats worked on writing in a more concrete and personal style— a style which would characterise his later poetry and which was a hallmark of modernism. As he was leaving, Yeats told Lady Gregory that he would be sorry to leave the peace of Stone Cottage, adding that it had been 'the best winter I have had in years . . . the only winter in which my creative power has been a conscious pleasure'. Yeats paid further visits in 1915, and again in the winter of 1915–16, when Pound was working on Ernest Fenollosa's translations of Japanese Noh plays. Yeats used elements of Japanese Noh in writing his first dance play *At the Hawk's Well* and wrote an introduction to Pound's *Certain noble plays of Japan*, published by Cuala Press in September 1916. Writing in 1935 about the time at Stone Cottage, Yeats claimed that Pound 'was the necessary critical audience compelling me to be objective'.

Responsibilities

On 25 May 1914 *Responsibilities* was published by Cuala Press. Yeats's anger at what he saw as the increasing philistinism of Irish life is apparent in the occasional poems about the Municipal Art Gallery published in various newspapers and previously collected in the volume *Poems written in discouragement*. On a more personal level, the 'Introductory rhymes' begged the pardon of his ancestors for the fact that, at 49, he remained unmarried and childless, blaming it on a 'barren passion'. There are poems concerning Maud Gonne and Iseult, including 'To a child dancing in the wind'. The poem 'Friends' praised three women in his life: Olivia Shakespear, Lady Gregory and Maud Gonne. In the last lines of the 'Closing rhymes' he anticipated how his growing antagonism towards modern Ireland would progress 'till all my priceless things / Are but a post the passing dogs defile'. The volume also included a new version of his play *The hour-glass*.

Stone Cottage, where WBY
stayed with Ezra Pound

To a friend who has asked me to sign his
manifesto to the neutral nations.

I think it better that at times like these
A poet keeps his mouth shut, for in truth
we have no gift to set a statesman right
He has had his fill, meddlin, who can please
A young girl in the indolence of her youth
Or an old man upon a winters night.

WBY. Feb 6. 1915

1915

Death of Hugh Lane

On 7 May 1915 Hugh Lane was among those who drowned when the Lusitania was sunk by a German submarine off the south coast of Ireland. Disappointed with the Dublin Corporation's 'want of public spirit' in its failure to provide a permanent gallery for the paintings he had presented, Lane had changed his will in 1913 and left some of the paintings to London instead of Dublin. Although Lane added a codicil in February 1915, stating that the paintings were to come to Dublin after all, it was not witnessed. The search for more a conclusive will involved several séances, where Yeats and Lady Gregory spoke to Lane's spirit. Contention over Lane's wishes led to a long-running dispute between rival claimants in Dublin and London, and Yeats and Lady Gregory ran several campaigns over the following years to try and ensure the return of the paintings to Dublin, which eventually succeeded.

Hugh Lane

Abbey debts

Despite its artistic successes the debts of the Abbey Theatre continued to grow, and in March 1915 Yeats considered closing the Theatre for the duration of the war. In December he gave a lecture entitled, 'The Irish theatre and other matters', which raised £200 to help relieve the Abbey's finances.

SOLOMON GREW WISE

Surely among a rich man's flowering lawns,

Amid the rustle of his planted hills,

Life overflows without ambitious pains;

And rains down life until the basin spills,

And mounts more dizzy high the more it rains

As though to choose whatever shape it wills

And never stoop to a mechanical

Or servile shape, at others' beck and call.

MEDITATIONS IN TIME
OF CIVIL WAR

At the Hawk's Well

On 2 April 1916 *At the Hawk's Well* was performed for the first time in London. It was the first of Yeats's dance plays in which he mixed elements of Japanese Noh drama with other theatrical and ritual elements. By March 1916 he was preparing a production of the play with the Japanese dancer Michio Ito and the designer Edmund Dulac, and the first performance took place in the dining room of Lady Cunard's house on Cavendish Square, London. The performance was repeated for charity two days later before a large audience that included Queen Alexandra.

'Easter 1916'

The 1916 Rising took Yeats by surprise. He was in England, staying with a friend, Sir William Rothenstein, in Gloucestershire, when it happened. His first reaction to the Rising appears to have been sadness at being away from Ireland when many of his acquaintances were dying. He was frustrated by the difficulty of getting accurate news about the events. But on 11 May, a few weeks after the Rising and after the execution of many of its leaders, he wrote to Lady Gregory, saying, 'I am trying to write a poem on the men executed—"terrible beauty has been born again".'

Completed by September 1916, this poem was privately printed by Clement Shorter, but Yeats feared that its publication would have a detrimental effect on other projects such as the pursuit of the Lane pictures. He was even told in September that his apparently pro-German stance might jeopardise his Civil List pension. 'Easter 1916' was published for the first time in the *New Statesman* on 23 October 1920. The poem, told in a direct and personal style, expressed Yeats's mixture of admiration and dismay at the Rising, and made use of his typical antinomies, especially in the much-quoted line, 'A terrible beauty is born.'

Michio Ito in *At the Hawk's Well*, 1916

Manuscript of 'Sixteen dead men'

Maud and Iseult Gonne

Maud Gonne's estranged husband John MacBride was among those executed early in May following the Easter Rising. On a visit to London, Iseult Gonne invited Yeats to France to look after her mother. Through the medium Elizabeth Radcliffe, Yeats consulted spirit guides on whether or not to ask Maud Gonne to marry him, and he continued to see Iseult in London during June. He finally secured permission to travel to France at the end of June, but Maud Gonne yet again refused his proposal of marriage. He stayed with the Gonnes in Normandy until the end of August, spending much time with Iseult Gonne, to whom he also proposed marriage. Though she refused his proposal, he continued to take an active interest in her over the coming years, and images of her from this time recur in several of his poems.

Reveries over childhood and youth

Reveries over childhood and youth, the first volume of Yeats's autobiographical writing, was published by Cuala Press in March 1916, though copies of it were available as early as December 1915. He had been working on it since 1914, occasionally discussing it with his sister Lily, who was the unofficial family historian and archivist. Yeats started to revise the Cuala edition while he was in Normandy with the Gonnes in July 1916. At this time he had already made substantial progress with the drafting of the next instalment of his autobiographies and, although he read parts of it to Maud and Iseult Gonne at the time, this second section was not published until October 1922.

PREFACE

Sometimes when I remember a relative that I have been fond of, or a strange incident of the past, I wander here and there till I have somebody to talk to. Presently I notice that my listener is bored; but now that I have written it out, I may even begin to forget it all. In any case, because one can always close a book, my friend need not be bored.

I have changed nothing to my knowledge; and yet it must be that I have changed many things without my knowledge, for I am writing after many ... friend nor letter ... t comes oftenest

... g friend of my ... different shape

... as Day, 1914.

REVERIES OVER CHILDHOOD AND
YOUTH BY WILLIAM BUTLER YEATS

MONOCEROS DE ASTRIS

THE CUALA PRESS
CHURCHTOWN
DUNDRUM
MCMXV

The title page of *Reveries over childhood and youth*

Iseult Gonne. Pastel by Maud Gonne

1917

Thoor Ballylee

In January 1917 Yeats wrote to the Congested Districts Board outlining terms for the purchase of a Norman tower at Ballylee, which had been known locally as Ballylee Castle and which Yeats named Thoor Ballylee (i.e., Ballylee Tower), using an Irish form of the name. He had started negotiating with the Board in October 1916 while staying at Coole writing 'The wild swans at Coole'. He finally bought the tower in March 1917 for £35, the amount of his inheritance from his uncle Alfred Pollexfen, though the inheritance had already been spent on membership of the Savile Club, to which he had just been elected. Architect William Scott organised renovations to the tower, which proved slow and expensive. Though it was significant in his personal life and his view of himself as a poet, and as a symbol in his poetry, the tower proved increasingly impractical and was closed down in October 1928. It was restored in the 1960s and now houses a Yeats museum. A number of poems, including 'A prayer on going into my house' and 'To be carved on a stone at Thoor Ballylee', refer to the tower, and it is the key symbol in the volumes *The tower* (1928) and *The winding stair* (1929; 1933).

Marriage

On 20 October 1917 Yeats married the 25-year-old Georgina (Georgie) Hyde Lees. She was the daughter of Edith Ellen (Nelly) Tucker, whose second husband, Harry Tucker, was Olivia Shakespear's brother. Her best friend was Dorothy Shakespear, Olivia's daughter, who had married Ezra Pound in April 1914. Yeats had been Pound's best man. George, as Yeats called her, was intellectual. Unlike Yeats himself, she was musical and a good linguist, and was inclined to cosmopolitan and bohemian life. Yeats had met her occasionally through their common interest in occult and psychic phenomena; in 1913 she had helped him with some

The Square

A Prayer on going into my house

God grant a blessing on this tower & cottage
and on my heirs, if all remain unspoiled,
No table or chair or stool not simple enough
For shepherds lads in Galilee; and grant
That I myself for portions of the year
May handle nothing and set eyes on nothing
But what the great and passionate have used
Throughout so many varying centuries
We take it for the norm; yet should I dream
Sinbad the sailor had brought a painted chest
Or image, from beyond the Loadstone Mountain
That dream is a norm; and should some limb of the Devil
Destroy the view by cutting down

Thoor Ballylee

Mrs W.B. Yeats.
Painting by
Edmund Dulac
(opposite)

research into a medium who produced automatic writing and in July 1914 he had sponsored her initiation into the Golden Dawn. It seems that Yeats had some powerful astrological motivation to marry and during the summer he proposed to Iseult Gonne who refused him. He proposed to George in September and she accepted. The wedding was at Harrow Road Register Office. Ezra Pound was best man and Dorothy Pound and Nelly Tucker were the only witnesses.

Yeats remained in the feverish emotional turmoil that had preceded his marriage for about a week, uncertain that he had made the right decision in marrying. Then, on 27 October, the situation changed. Yeats described how:

George spoke of the sensation of having lived through something before . . . Then she said she felt that something was to be written through her. She got a piece of paper, & talking to me all the while so that her thoughts would not effect [sic] what she wrote, wrote these words (which she did not understand) 'with the bird' (Iseult) 'all is well at heart . . .'

Yeats's pains and fever abated and 'From being more miserable than I ever remember being since Maud Gonne's marriage I became extremely happy.' This was the beginning of George's automatic writing, an exploration of occult ideas foreshadowed in *Per amica silentia lunae*, through which Yeats and George also got to know one another more deeply. Initially the messages Yeats sought were assurances about Iseult and Maud, but George's spirit controls and instructors offered other advice too—for instance, encouraging them to conceive a child. George's spirits were providing the information that formed the basis for the system developed in *A vision*.

The restoration of Yeats's faith in Irish idealism, his marriage, and George's automatic writing provided him with energy, which enabled him to enjoy a great new period of creativity beginning at about this time. From 1917 onwards Yeats began to find new ways of thinking and of writing, and these were to lead to the great achievements of the second half of his life.

George Yeats (left) and (above) with WBY in New York, 1920

SOLOMON GREW WISE

The wild swans at Coole

On 17 November 1917 *The wild swans at Coole* was published by Cuala Press. The Cuala Press edition contained 28 poems, as well as the play *At the Hawk's Well*. Among the poems were 'The wild swans at Coole', 'The fisherman', 'Lines written in dejection', and the sequence of seven poems about Mabel Beardsley entitled 'Upon a dying lady'. For the Macmillan edition of March 1919, Yeats added a further 16 poems, including 'In memory of Major Robert Gregory', 'An Irish airman foresees his death', and 'The scholars'.

Oxford

In January 1918 Yeats and his wife George moved into a house at 45 Broad Street, Oxford. In October they moved to 4 Broad Street, described by Yeats in a letter to Lady Gregory as 'such a house as I love—all harmonious & severe, nothing looking expensive or too cheap but a dignified natural house for intellectual people'. Oxford held a number of attractions. Yeats was familiar with it from previous visits to the Bodleian Library, where he now researched references from George's automatic writing. There was also the company of the university intellectuals and others, like the writers Eleanor Jourdain and Anne Moberley, who had written about a strange experience at Versailles where they had slipped in time to the pre-Revolutionary period. At nearby Garsington Manor Yeats also found a convivial and intellectual atmosphere. Yeats had believed that George wanted to live in Oxford but she did not mix well with the dons' wives and by 1921 Yeats realised that she would rather live in Ireland. In 1921 the Yeatses decide to economise and let Broad Street, moving to Shillingford, 15 miles outside Oxford, and they later moved again to Cuttlebrook House in the village of Thame, where their son Michael Yeats was born.

The swans in Coole

The woods are in their autumn colours
    But the lake waters are low
~~The~~ ~~out our~~ path, ~~they~~ ~~and the~~ footfalls she
The path way has and is foot~~s~~
    ~~And~~ the in the pale twilight?
    In the ~~half dark~~ ~~to~~
~~indolence~~
~~indolent~~ away, the ~~shadow~~ the gues, the
~~and~~ as ~~number~~ the ~~swan~~, as number the ~~la~~
in ~~shadow~~, ~~sres~~, ~~two~~, as number the
in dolens away to stones a number the

    Thorins, amors, the stones.

we are now as the number autumn
    since I first made my count.
I make ~~in~~ so in the of the have in
    suddenly the lone mount
~~suddenly~~
at wheel above the ~~lake~~ in great broken rings
    and a slow clamour of ~~wings~~.
But now this ~~drops in~~ the stills water
    mysterious, beautiful
away that water our their eggs

Manuscript and book cover of *The wild swans at Coole*

SOLOMON GREW WISE

Per amica silentia lunae

In January 1918 *Per amica silentia lunae* was published by Macmillan. It is an essay in two parts: 'Anima hominis' and 'Anima mundi'—the human soul and the World's Soul. It had been written early in 1917 and was inspired by conversations Yeats had in Normandy in 1916 with Iseult Gonne, to whom it was dedicated (under her pseudonym 'Maurice'). The title was from Virgil and translates as 'through the friendly silences of the moon'. Themes in the book follow his interest in the spiritual and his philosophical reflections. Like his earlier book *Discoveries*, *Per amica silentia lunae* is composed of short sections, separate but linked, in a discursive style that is frequently aphoristic. It contains one of Yeats's best-known aphorisms: 'We make out of the quarrel with others, rhetoric, but of the quarrel with ourselves, poetry.' Elsewhere, he deals with ideas of recurrence ('all passionate moments recur again and again, for passion desires its own recurrence more than any event . . .'), and the Great Memory or World's Soul, musing upon the Cambridge Platonists and Shelley, the dead and the Condition of Fire. He also explores masks ('A poet, when he is growing old, will ask himself if he cannot keep his mask and his vision without new bitterness, new disappointment'), the anti-self, most notably in the poem 'Ego dominus tuus', which forms the essay's preface, and introduces the concept of the Daimon, with the figure of Leo Africanus obviously lurking beneath the surface:

a strange living man may win for Daimon an illustrious dead man . . . the Daimon comes not as like to like but seeking its own opposite, for man and Daimon feed the hunger of one another's hearts.

Per amica silentia lunae is in many ways the starting point for the automatic script and *A vision* and Yeats wrote in a rejected draft:

In Per Amica Silentia Lunae I have described the whole of human life as man's attempt to become the opposite of himself and to create the opposite of his fate, and if I were to judge by accepted psychology I would describe this system [A vision] as an elaboration by my wife's unconscious of those few crude sentences.

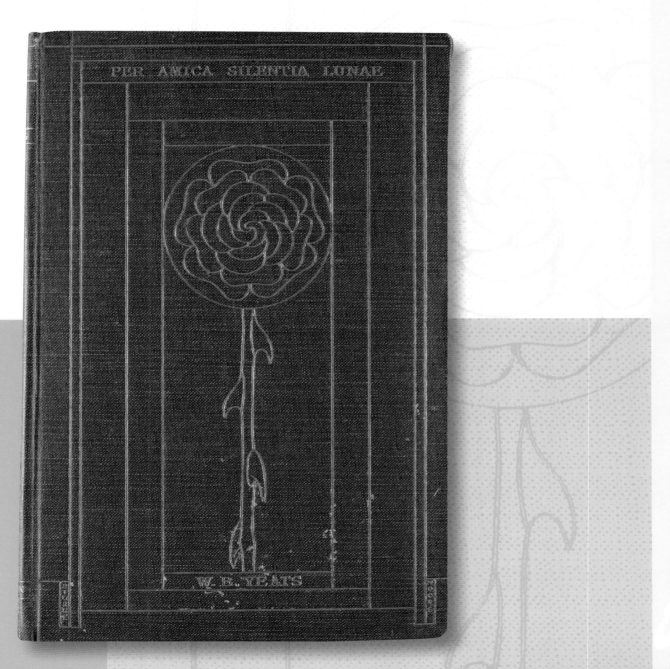

Book cover of
Per amica silentia lunae

The only jealousy of Emer

In January 1918 Yeats finished work on his second dance play, *The only jealousy of Emer*. He began writing the play in November 1917, a fortnight after his marriage, and the action of the play reflects the emotional turmoil he suffered at the time. The play was also inspired by concepts arising from George Yeats's automatic writing. In the play, Cuchulain's wife, his mistress and a supernatural woman from his past (symbolic figures but very close to George, Iseult Gonne and Maud Gonne) struggle to restore Cuchulain, whose soul has been taken over by an evil spirit. As he finished *The only jealousy of Emer*, Yeats had an idea for another play that became *Calvary*, a play that was not performed in his lifetime. *The only jealousy of Emer* was his third Cuchulain play.

Death of Robert Gregory

On 4 February 1918 Yeats heard from Lady Gregory that her son and the heir to the Coole estate, Robert, had been killed. He was a pilot in the Royal Air Force and had been shot down by friendly fire while returning from a mission in Italy. He had been buried in Padua. By 25 February, Yeats, at the subtle request of Lady Gregory, was working on an elegy, 'Shepherd and goatherd', which he finished in March. It was the first of four poems on Robert Gregory, including 'An Irish airman foresees his death', 'In memory of Major Robert Gregory' and 'Reprisals'. The latter poem was written in late 1921 about the reprisals of contending factions in the Anglo-Irish War. It was withheld from publication at Lady Gregory's request. She felt that Yeats was dragging her son from the grave for the sake of what she considered an insincere poem, though she did not tell him this.

IN MEMORY OF ROBERT GREGORY.

(Major Robert Gregory,R.F.C. M.C. Legion of Honour, was killed in action

on the Italian front, January 23, 1918)

Now that we're almost settled in our house
I'll name the friends that cannot sup with us
Beside a fire of turf in th'ancient tower,
And having talked to some late hour
Climb up the narrow winding stair to bed;
Discoverers of forgotten truth,Or mere companions of my youth,
All,all are in my thoughts tonight, being dead.

Always we's have the new friend meet the old
And we are hurt if either friend seem cold,
And there is salt to lengthen out the smart
In the affections of our heart,
And quarrels are blown up upon that head;
But not a friend that I would bring
This night, can set us quarrelling,
For all that come into my mind are dead.

Lionel Johnson comes the first to mind
That loved his learning better than mankind
Though courteous to the worst; much falling he
Brooded upon sanctity
Till all his Greek and Latin learning seemed
A long blast upon the horn that brought
A little nearer to his thought
A measureless consummation that he dreamed.

Lady Gregory's son
Robert, who was shot
down in 1918

Manuscript of 'In
memory of Major Robert
Gregory'

Birth of Anne Yeats

At 10 a.m. on 26 February 1919 Anne Butler Yeats was born prematurely. She was named after Anne Butler, *née* Hyde, wife of the second Duke of Ormonde, who had died at Dublin Castle on 25 January 1685 after a miscarriage. George Yeats had received messages from the spirit of Anne Butler, in March 1918, suggesting that she and Yeats should conceive a child who would be the reincarnation of Anne Butler's miscarried son. After Anne's birth, in March 1919, Yeats wrote 'A prayer for my daughter', finishing the poem at Thoor Ballylee in June. It was published in the *Irish Statesman* on 8 November 1919. He and George Yeats spent a couple of days at the beginning of July in Kilkenny, ancestral home of the Dukes of Ormonde, looking for Anne Butler's grave.

Departure from Woburn Buildings

In June 1919 Yeats gave up the lease on Woburn Buildings, which had been his home in London for 23 years. It had become too expensive to maintain along with his house in Oxford and Thoor Ballylee in Ireland.

'A people's theatre'

In November 1919 Yeats gave a lecture entitled, 'The people's theatre' at the Oxford University Dramatic Society, and his open letter to Lady Gregory bearing the same title was published in two parts in the *Irish Statesman* on 29 November and 6 December 1919. Under a title borrowed from Romain Rolland, Yeats set out his ideas on the kind of theatre he wanted:

I want to create for myself an unpopular theatre and an audience like a secret society where admission is by favour and never too many . . . I want so much—an audience of fifty, a room worthy of it (some great dining-room or drawing-room), half a dozen young men and women who can dance and speak verse or play drum and flute and zither, and all the while, instead of a profession,

A PRAYER FOR MY DAUGHTER.

I.

Once more the storm is howling and half hid
Under this cradle hood and coverlid
My child sleeps on.   There is no obstacle
But Gregory's Woods and one bare hill
Whereby the haystack and roof-levelling wind
Bred on the Atlantic can be stayed
And for an hour I have walked and **prayed**
Because of the great gloom that is in my mind;

II.

I have walked and **prayed** for this young child an hour
And heard the sea-wind scream **upon the tower,**
And under the arches of the bridge, and scream
In the elms above the flooded stream;
Imagining in excited reverie
That the future years had come
Dancing to a frenzied drum
Out of the murderous innocence of the sea.

III.

be granted beauty and yet not
s to make a stranger's eye distraught,
before a looking-glass, for such,
de beautiful overmuch,
beauty as sufficient end,
tural kindness and maybe
rt-revealing intimacy,
ooses **right,** and never find a friend.

WBY with his daughter Anne

AYER FOR MY DAUGHTER

I

the storm is howling and half hid
cradle-hood and coverlid
sleeps on.   There is no obstacle
ry's Woods and one bare hill
he haystack and roof-levelling wind,
e Atlantic, can be stayed;
hour I have walked and prayed
the great gloom that is in my mind.

II

ed and prayed for this young child an hour
the sea-wind scream upon the tower,
the arches of the bridge, and scream
s above the flooded stream ;
in excited reverie
ature years had come,
a frenzied drum,
murderous innocence of the sea.

III

e granted beauty and yet not
make a stranger's eye distraught,
fore a looking-glass, for such,
beautiful overmuch,
beauty a sufficient end,
al kindness and maybe
revealing intimacy
es right, and never find a friend.

IV

VII

My mind because the minds that I have loved,
The sort of beauty that I have approved,
Prosper but little, has dried up of late,
Yet knows that to be choked with hate
May well be of all evil chances chief.
If there's no hatred in a mind
Assault and battery of the wind
Can never tear the linnet from the leaf.

VIII

An intellectual hatred is the worst,
So let her think opinions are accursed.
Have I not seen the loveliest woman born
Out of the mouth of Plenty's horn,
Because of her opinionated mind
Barter that horn and every good
By quiet natures understood
For an old bellows full of angry wind ?

IX

Considering that, all hatred driven hence,
The soul recovers radical innocence
And learns at last that it is self-delighting,
Self-appeasing, self-affrighting,
And that its own sweet will is heaven's will,
She can, though every face should scowl
And every windy quarter howl
Or every bellows burst, be happy still.

X

And may her bride-groom bring her to a house
Where all's accustomed, ceremonious ;
For arrogance and hatred are the wares
Peddled in the thoroughfares.
How but in custom and in ceremony
Are innocence and beauty born ?
Ceremony's a name for the rich horn,

SOLOMON GREW WISE

I but offer them 'an accomplishment.' ['Accomplishment' here is the English translation of the Japanese 'Noh'.] *I desire a mysterious art, always reminding and half-reminding those who understand it of dearly loved things, doing its work by suggestion, not by direct statement, a complexity of rhythm, colour, gesture, not space-pervading like the intellect, but a memory and a prophecy . . .*

Michael Robartes and the dancer

In February 1921 *Michael Robartes and the dancer* was published by Cuala Press. In this book Yeats's poems on the 1916 Easter Rising ('Sixteen dead men', The rose tree', and 'On a political prisoner') were published for the first time, along with 'Easter 1916', which had been previously published in the *New Statesman*. The period after his marriage had been particularly productive and a number of the poems in this book addressed his wife George ('Solomon and the witch', 'An image from a past life', 'Under Saturn', 'Towards break of day' and 'Demon and beast'). Many also made use of the occult imagery developed through George's automatic writing. 'The second coming', for instance, was written early in 1919 and used imagery from the automatic writing to reflect on the destructive turn of world events. There were also poems to his newborn daughter ('A prayer for my daughter') and for the tower at Ballylee ('To be carved on a stone at Thoor Ballylee').

ng aloft a specimen of his ware, " will
. It cost me a shilling, and I am pre-
it to you for two shillings. I am not
profiteers of whom you read in the
ry one *per cent* is sufficient for my modest
y friend, for whose integrity I have
asks me to believe that the genius was
a few minutes—and Portadown is still
l. I think he deserved his success, and
the incident for careful study to those
no are considering the fiscal provisions
ernment with relation to the granting of
uards to Ulster; in Portadown at least
ously needed.

———

l of democratic ideas does not appear to
ct on the arbitrary standard of respect
rded to titles and distinctions, however
ned. The American papers are filled
ment that the Prince of Wales can lay
onet and robes—or is it feathers?—long
take a dive in the swimming pool." It
so that he walks and talks like an ordinary
tice, too, that a gentleman has just been
an English University with the degree
Arts, because he commanded the Officers'
rps—which seems a gross injustice to
ave hitherto paid for this honour in hard
nally I should not feel greatly elevated
if the War Office made me an honorary
ny prowess in these pages, but I do not
any of my acquaintance would soon come
as a proof of my military efficiency and
nswer to that depressing question which,
the posters, our grandchildren will learn
In all seriousness, I hope that the new
he future will not fall a victim to this
ch is worse than open snobbery. That
c constitution offers no safeguards against
by American precedent. I knew a man
troduced in the streets of an American
ly who bore the title of Mrs. Forecaster
r husband had won his title by services
weather bureau. Besides such a table of
role of precedence of a European Court
significance. Let us have no Geheimerats.

———

ceived through the courtesy of the gentle-
arge of this matter a full account of the
of the United States Department of
in the recovery of potash and other by-
m kelp. So far the experiments, conducted
war on a large scale, appear to have been
sful. As to the possibility of establishing
process over here my authority writes:

recovered economically." Here is an opportunity for
investigation, and, perhaps, for action, by the Com-
mission of Enquiry into Industrial Resources; it
seems quite possible that we have a large supply of
valuable raw material going to waste while we import
expensive articles which could be produced from it.
SIGMA.

A PEOPLE'S THEATRE:

A LETTER TO LADY GREGORY

I.

MY DEAR LADY GREGORY:

Of recent years you have done all that is anxious
and laborious in the supervision of the Abbey Theatre
and left me free to follow my own thoughts. It is
therefore right that I address to you this letter,
wherein I shall explain, half for your ears, half for
other ears, certain thoughts that have made me believe
that the Abbey Theatre can never do all we had hoped.
We set out to make a "People's Theatre" and in
that we have succeeded. But I did not know until
very lately that there are certain things, dear to both
our hearts, which no "People's Theatre" can
accomplish.

II.

All exploitation of the life of the wealthy, for the
eye and the ear of the poor and half poor, in plays, in
popular novels, in musical comedy, in fashion papers,
at the cinema, in *Daily Mirror* photographs, is a
travesty of the life of the rich; and if it were not
would all but justify some red terror; and it im-
poverishes and vulgarises the imagination, seeming to
hold up for envy and to commend a life where all is
display and hurry, passion without emotion, emotion
without intellect, and where there is nothing stern and
solitary. The plays and novels are the least mis-
chievous, for they still have old-fashioned romanticism
—their threepenny bit, if worn, is silver yet—but
they are without intensity and intellect and cannot in
those they would represent convey the charm of
either. All this exploitation is a rankness that has
grown up recently among us and has come out of an
historical necessity that has made the furniture and
the clothes and the brains, of all but the leisured or
the lettered, copies and travesties.

Shakespeare set upon the stage Kings and Queens,
great historical or legendary persons about whom all
was reality, except the circumstance of their lives
which remain vague and summary because, his mind
and the mind of his audience being interested in
emotion and intellect at their moment of union and
at their greatest intensity, he could only write his best

549

understanding the clock,
tre of Shakespeare or
had told you how at
the like, young men
papers to one another
and you yourself soon
then but a new weak
At Spiddal or near
Gaelic songs, all new
rature had naivety and
nothing for cleverness,
gic or humorous, and
f of a Girl's Heart,"
the same speech and
know that the songs
but these, in the age
ame relation to great
ngs were as unlike as
Hall with their clever
k of some mind as
or or of a newspaper
ld bring the old folk-
o aid us, and with the
understanding heart,
, as the most interior

wilderness, that which we observe through our senses
and that which we can experience only, and our art is
always the description of one or the other. If our art
is mainly from experience we have need of learned
speech, of agreed symbols, because all those things
whose names renew experience, have accompanied that
experience already many times. A personage in one of
Turgenev's novels is reminded by the odour of, I think,
heliotrope, of some sweetheart that had worn it, and
poetry is any flower that brings a memory of emotion,
while an unmemoried flower is prose, and a flower

Being; but the modern world is more powerful than
any Propaganda or even than any special circumstance, and our success has been that we have made a
Theatre of the head, and persuaded Dublin playgoers
to think about their own trade or profession or class
and their life within it, so long as the stage curtain is
up, in relation to Ireland as a whole. For certain
hours of an evening they have objective modern eyes.

W. B. YEATS.

(To be continued.)

WBY's open letter to Lady Gregory entitled 'A people's theatre' which was published in two parts in the *Irish Statesman*

SOLOMON GREW WISE

Oxford Union speech

On 17 February 1921 Yeats made a speech at the Oxford Union in which he denounced British policy in Ireland, particularly the actions of the Black and Tans. He had been invited by James O'Reilly to address the University's Irish Society, and the Oxford Union also sent him an invitation. After his address to the Irish Society on 16 February, he told O'Reilly that he would tell the Oxford Union debate that the King's soldiers in Ireland were murderers. Reports from all sides of the Union debate agree that his performance was electrifying. He spoke for what Reilly called 'twelve minutes of bitter and blazing attack on the English in Ireland'. Yeats claimed that not the law, but English law, had broken down in Ireland. He said there was a lot of talk about law and liberty but also truth in the gibe that the war had made the world safe for hypocrisy. His speech was cheered by all present and the motion, welcoming complete self-government in Ireland and condemning reprisals, was carried by 219 to 129. No document of the speech survives, since Yeats spoke without a script.

'All Souls' Night'

On 5 March 1921 the poem 'All Souls' Night' was published in the *London Mercury*. Yeats had started work on it at Broad Street, Oxford, in September 1920. It commemorates several occult friends who had died in recent years: W.H. Horton (d. 1919) and his partner Audrey Locke (d. 1916), Florence Farr (d. 1917) and MacGregor Mathers (d. 1918). It was reprinted later as the epilogue of *A vision*.

Birth of Michael Yeats

On 22 August 1921 Michael Butler Yeats was born at Thame, outside Oxford. He was christened on December 20 with Lennox Robinson as his godfather. Ottoline Morrell was among others present for the christening and celebrations afterwards.

TWO PLAYS FOR DANCERS
BY W. B. YEATS

MONOCEROS DE ASTRIS

WBY with his family
(from left: Anne, George,
WBY and Michael)

1922

Death of John Butler Yeats

On 3 February Yeats's father, John Butler Yeats, died in New York aged 83. With no income of his own, John Butler Yeats had been persuaded to write letters that could be published, and Ezra Pound had edited a first selection of letters, published by Cuala Press in 1917. Another selection edited by Lennox Robinson appeared in 1920. However, John Butler Yeats remained financially dependent on his family and on friends like John Quinn, and for some time they had tried to persuade him to return to Ireland. A one-way ticket had been booked for November 1921; then the date was changed to December, but John Butler Yeats had stubbornly refused to leave New York.

Merrion Square

In September Yeats and his family moved into 82 Merrion Square. It remained the family home for almost six years. Situated close to the government headquarters in Dublin's city centre, it became a target as the Civil War continued. In October 1922 a bomb exploded nearby, cracking a window in the house, and on Christmas Eve shots were fired through the windows, injuring George Yeats.

WBY's father,
John Butler Yeats
(self-portrait)

82 Merrion Square,
home of the Yeats family
for six years

Irish Civil War

The ratification of the Anglo-Irish Treaty by the Dáil in January 1922 precipitated the Irish Civil War. Eamon de Valera's Republican forces fought the forces of the newly established Free State until April 1923, when the death of Liam Lynch, Chief of Staff, effectively ended Republican resistance.

By June 1922 Yeats had started work on a long poem that later became 'Meditations in time of civil war', first published in the *London Mercury* in January 1923. He and his family were directly threatened by the Civil War. The bridge at Thoor Ballylee was blown up in August 1922, resulting in damage to the tower, and Yeats's home at Merrion Square came under gunfire. Republicans issued threats against the lives and homes of all who participated in the Free State government—including Yeats, who accepted his nomination by the Taoiseach, William Cosgrave, to the Senate in December 1922.

SMILING PUBLIC MAN

What shall I do with this absurdity—
O heart, O troubled heart—this caricature,
Decrepit age that has been tied to me
As to a dog's tail?
                    Never had I more
Excited, passionate, fantastical
Imagination, nor an ear and eye
That more expected the impossible . . .

THE TOWER

1923

Nobel Prize

On 14 November 1923 Yeats heard from Bertie Smyllie of the *Irish Times* that he had been awarded the Nobel Prize for Literature. It is said that Yeats's first reaction was to ask Smyllie how much the prize was worth. In his statements following the announcement of the award, Yeats made it clear that this was an honour for Ireland. He said, 'I consider that this honour has come to me less as an individual than as a representative of Irish literature. It is part of Europe's welcome to the Free State.' In December Yeats and George travelled to Stockholm where he was presented with the medal and parchment by King Gustav V on 10 December. The Swedish Royal Theatre gave a performance of *Cathleen ni Houlihan* in his honour a few days later. Yeats later recorded his reactions to the award and his Swedish visit in *The bounty of Sweden*, published in 1924. The prize amounted to £6,800. Yeats used £800 to pay off some of the debts at Cuala Press and invested the rest.

1924

Sean O'Casey

Juno and the paycock premiered at the Abbey in March 1924.

O'Casey's first play, *The crimson in the tri-colour*, had been rejected by the Abbey in 1922, but he was encouraged by Lady Gregory and went on to write plays that proved very successful at the Abbey and internationally. *Juno and the paycock* was followed by *The plough and the stars* in February 1926, which proved particularly controversial. Even greater controversy was to follow with the Abbey's rejection of O'Casey's *The silver tassie* in 1928.

MR. YEATS IN STOCKHOLM.

RECEIVES NOBEL PRIZE.

PRESENTED BY THE KING OF SWEDEN.

STOCKHOLM, Monday.

The award of the Nobel Prizes to-day, on the anniversary of the death of the donor, was the occasion of the customary public ceremony, at which the King and several members of the Royal Family were present.

As the 1922-23 prizes for medicine were both awarded on this occasion, and were both divided into two shares, the total number of recipients this year is seven, instead of four, and of these four were present to-day—namely, Dr. Pregl, of Graz (Chemistry); Dr. Hill, of London, and Dr. Meyerhof, of Kiel (Medicine, 1922); and Mr. W. B. Yeats (Literature).

The other recipients are Dr. Milligan, of Washington (Physics); Dr. Banting and Dr. MacLeod, of Canada (Medicine, 1923).

After the prizes had been presented by the King a banquet was held, under the presidency of Prince William.—(Reuter.)

MYSTERY OF SEA

DEAD BODIES ON BOA

On the arrival of th at Southampton yes Captain Thomas, her skippe when about five miles south Sunday morning he sighted a of the steamer Rosa, which foundered in heavy seas.

When they got alongside discovered that it contained f Almost immediately, howev capsized, and when it righte bodies remained. The others on the surface.

Captain Thomas towed t the two bodies to Southampt quest will be held.

The deceased men have no nor is anything definitely Rosa's fate.

The steamer Innisholm bel Shipping company, Cardiff.

The Rosa, an iron screw st gross, belonged to Messrs. R London.

PRISONER R

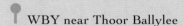

WBY near Thoor Ballylee

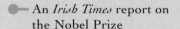

An *Irish Times* report on the Nobel Prize

Sean O'Casey (opposite)

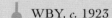

WBY, *c.* 1923

1925

The National Theatre

In July 1925 the Free State government decided to give an annual subsidy to the Abbey Theatre, making it the first state-endowed theatre in the English-speaking world. The event was celebrated on 8 August with a dinner for Ernest Blythe on the stage of the Abbey, during which Yeats spoke on the history of the Abbey. Relations between government and theatre were not always easy, but the award of the subsidy indicated the significance accorded to the achievement of the Abbey by the government of the new state.

Divorce debate

In June 1925 Yeats caused controversy with his intervention in a Senate debate on a law prohibiting divorce. In his speech he warned, 'Once you attempt legislation on religious grounds you open up the way for every kind of intolerance and for every kind of religious persecution.' Perhaps as a counter to Catholic pieties current at this time, Yeats wrote the poem 'The three monuments', in which he alluded to the scandalous reputations of Daniel O'Connell, Lord Nelson and Charles Stewart Parnell, whose monuments all stood on O'Connell Street at the time. Yeats's divorce speech is included in the Yeats Collection.

Ottoline Morrell

In December 1925 Yeats spent a weekend at Garsington Manor, home of Lady Ottoline Morrell, where he met Ethel Sands, Edward Sackville-West and Gilbert Spencer (who provided the illustrations for Yeats's 'Three things') among others. Between his first visit in 1919 and his quarrel with Ottoline Morrell in 1937 he often visited Garsington and the Morrells' London home at Gower Street. Through Ottoline Morrell he met many of the important personalities of the day, including Bertrand Russell, David Cecil, L.A.G. Strong, Virginia Woolf, Walter de la Mare and Dorothy Wellesley. He wrote the poem 'Spilt milk' on 8 November 1930, the day after a discussion with Morrell and Walter de la Mare, recorded by Virginia Woolf who was also present. The gardens at Garsington are recalled in the first part of 'Meditations in time of civil war'.

June 10.1925-

I shall vote against the resolution sent up
because ~ have any special interest in the syb
se I consider the resolution and act of aggres
to assume - it was indeed declared in some ma
olic Truth Society at a meeting of the Catholic
Catholic would avail himself of opportunities f
and therefore what President Cosgrave proposes
Church of Ireland, and men of no Church, who do
be forbidden it.   President Cosgrave and the
for I legislate in a matter that does not concern them al...
ity, and   doubt that if they possess
they would legislate with the same confidence
ollowers of Confucius, and even prhaps with pe
st those members of their own faith who in va
e have assisted their non-Catholic neighbours
xious to the purer faith of Ireland.   It is
quixotic indeed that one has to seek its like
onder however if they have calculated the cost
wonder that, for an enthusiasm so perfect woul
never calculated th...
no matter what the cost.   We
press the matter on their

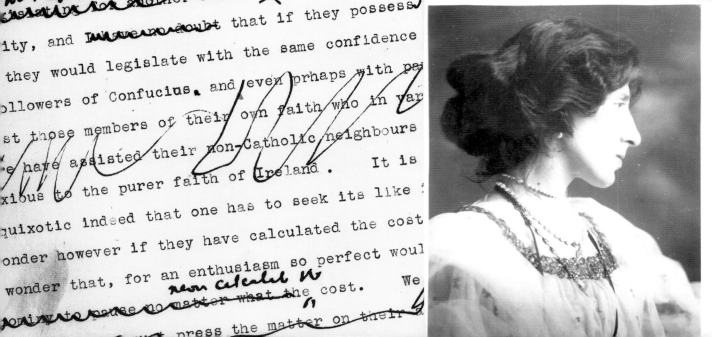

page one hundred and thirty-one

A vision

On 15 January 1926 *A vision* was published by Werner Laurie in 600 copies signed by Yeats (the book is dated 1925). Subtitled, 'An explanation of life founded upon the writings of Giraldus and upon certain doctrines attributed to Kusta ben Luka', *A vision* was Yeats's effort to systematise the material of George Yeats's automatic writing. It was couched, however, in an Arabian fiction and further framed with a story about Michael Robartes and Owen Aherne concerning the discovery of the material, thus disguising George's part in it. Yeats dedicated the book to 'Vestigia', Moina Mathers's occult name. In the dedication he claims that 'truth cannot be discovered but may be revealed, and that if a man does not lose faith, and if he go through certain preparations, revelation will find him at the fitting moment'.

The system outlined in the automatic script and in *A vision* is based on a cycle that moves from unity through separation into multiplicity, back to absorption into unity and so on. The cycle is symbolised by two intersecting cones or gyres and by the phases of the moon; it is traced in nature, human history, the many incarnations of a soul, and the individual life and afterlife. Unity is associated with God, society, the mass, spirituality and objectivity, while multiplicity is the Daimon, the individual, loneliness, creativity and subjectivity.

Yeats was not satisfied with the book and began revising it in 1927. The second edition, with a large portion completely rewritten, was published in October 1937.

O'Casey controversy

In February 1926 Yeats and the Abbey Theatre became embroiled in controversy over Sean O'Casey's play *The plough and the stars*. There were objections to the play's critical attitude to the 1916 Rising and, even more so, to the association of the character Rosie Redmond, a prostitute, with the (by now sacred) event. In short, the familiar objection to an unfavourable portrayal of Irish sexual morals in a play was once again firing an Abbey row.

The Works of W. B. Yeats

A VISION

By

W. B. YEATS

A revised and amplified version of an
important book which has not hitherto been
available to the general public, setting forth
the esoteric principles, doctrines, and experiences from which much of Mr. Yeats's most
notable work in poetry and prose derives its
inspiration and significance.

MACMILLAN AND CO. LTD.

Book cover of *A vision*

WBY arriving at
the Seanad

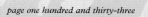

SMILING PUBLIC MAN

The controversy had started in September 1925, when an emergency meeting of the Abbey directors had to be called and resulted in the introduction of majority voting for such meetings. By January 1926, some of the actors were refusing to say certain lines, and O'Casey withdrew the play temporarily. The opening night on 8 February 1926 caused further controversy, and Republicans rushed the stage at the performance on 11 February. The police were called and Yeats denounced the audience from the stage, in the famous line, 'You have disgraced yourselves again.' Performances continued under police protection when threats were made against individual actors and against the Abbey.

'Among school children'

On 21 March 1926 Yeats lunched with the Sisters of Mercy at St Otteran's School, Waterford, and the following day he conducted an inspection of the school, run according to Maria Montessori's principles. These events provide the context for his poem 'Among school children'. Yeats was becoming concerned about education policy and methods in the new state, and on 24 March he spoke in the Senate on the School Attendance Bill, pleading for a wide range of innovative measures to assist children. He was reading works on education by Benedetto Croce, the Italian philosopher, who resisted rationalism and materialism and was devoted to a poetic vision of the world, and whose theories, although he was opposed to Fascism, were being used in Mussolini's Italy. Yeats was also reading works by Giovanni Gentile, Minister for Education in Mussolini's government, whose ideas on education were popular in Ireland in the 1920s. It was around this time that Yeats wrote the poem 'Father and child' about his daughter Anne.

Committee on Coinage

In May 1926 Yeats was appointed chairman of the Committee on Coinage, entrusted with finding designs for new Free State coins. He chaired the first meeting of the Committee in June 1926, and in February 1927 it chose designs by English artist Percy Metcalfe, based on images

what we did or tried to c[...]

by W B Yeats Chairman of [...]

I.

As the most famous and beautiful [...]
of the Greek Colonies, especially of those in [...]
and one
to send photographs of some of these coins of [...]
selected artists and to ask them as far as pos[...]
as a model.   But the Greek coins had two adv[...]
could not have, one side need not balance the [...]
could be stamped in high relief, whereas ours must pitch and spin
to please the gambler, and pack into rolls to please   the banker.

II.

We asked advice as to [...]
by the public Round Towers, wolfh[...]
wreaths, and the Treaty Stone of [...] a advi[...]
Society of Antiquaries To avoid [...] mblems altogether[...]
even the Shamrock emblem was not [...] years old.   We would
have avoided them in any case [...] d to choose such forms as
permit an artist to display [...] apacity for design and
expression, and as Ireland i[...] the first modern State to design
an entire coinage, not one [...] in nov[...] another years later, as
old dies wore out or the pu[...] changed its taste, it seemed best
to give the coins some relation to one another.   The most

SEANAD EIREANN.

DEC 1922

TICEUD SEANADÓRA

Ainm   *W. B. Yeats*

Emmet Dalton

Cléireach an tSeanaid

WBY's Seanad pass

This picture was circulated
to members of the
Committee on Coinage
Designs

Coinage Committee
report on new coins

page one hundred and thirty-five

of wild and domestic animals found in Ireland. This proved a controversial decision for several reasons (including the fact that Metcalfe was English, and also that farmers' organisations felt the animals were badly represented and a poor advertisement for Irish livestock). In August 1927 Yeats went to Coole to write up the Committee's report. Photographs of the new designs reached him at Coole in August 1928 when he dictated an essay on them to Lady Gregory. James MacNeill brought a set of the new coins to him at Rapallo later in 1928. The designs remained the basis for Irish coins until the introduction of the Euro in 2002.

Broadcasting

On 2 September 1926 *The land of heart's desire* was broadcast on radio in a production by BBC Belfast. This was the first of many such broadcasts of Yeats's plays and poetry over the coming years by the BBC at Belfast and London. On 8 September 1931 Yeats made his first radio broadcast, reading a selection of his poems in a programme broadcast by BBC Belfast.

Assassination of Kevin O'Higgins

On 10 July 1927 Free State Minister Kevin O'Higgins was shot outside his house on Cross Avenue, Blackrock, on his way to Mass. Yeats, who had met O'Higgins on several occasions, was deeply shocked by the assassination. An admirer of Mussolini, O'Higgins was nonetheless committed to parliamentary democracy, and his stance on law and order appealed to Yeats's conservatism. Though O'Higgins was instrumental in the introduction of censorship legislation that Yeats fought against, he joined Yeats's pantheon of leaders who, like Parnell, were not afraid to be unpopular. Yeats later called him 'the finest intellect in Irish public life, and . . . my friend'. Both Maud Gonne and her son Seán MacBride were interviewed about the assassination and she appealed to Yeats for help, salvaging their relationship. These events provide a context for his poems 'Death' and 'Blood and the moon', and for his elegy 'In memory of Eva Gore-Booth and Con Markiewicz'. Markiewicz had died in a Dublin hospital five days after O'Higgins.

1927

SAORSTÁT ÉIREANN
(IRISH FREE STATE).

Uimhir Thagartha
(Ref. No.)

OIFIG AN RÚNAÍ DO'N ÁRD CHOMH
(Office of the Secretary to the Executive Council

BAILE ÁTHA CLIA
(Dublin).

15th June, 1923.

Senator Yeats,
Merrion Square,
Dublin.

A Chara,

      The President mentioned to the Executive
Council your suggestion that it would be
desirable that the Government should avail itself
of the offer made by you, Sir John Lavery
and others, to act as an Advisory Committee
regarding Official Designs and I was instructed to
see you in connection with the matter so as to
go into the details of the proposal.

      I shall be glad therefore if you will
ly indicate a date and time most conven
ou for an appointment for this purpose.

        Mise le meas,

Diarmuid Ó Riger

Irish animals, wild and
domestic, featured in the
designs for the new coins

— Letter to WBY asking
him to sit on the Coinage
Committee and (below) a
list of other members

— Countess Markievicz

The Committee appointed to advise the Government on Coinage Designs

42 FITZWILLIAM SQUARE,
DUBLIN.
PHONE 61831.

Thomas Bodkin D. litt, Present Director of the National Gallery
Dermod O'Brien, President of the Royal Hibernian Academy
Lucius O'Callaghan, formerly Director of the National Gallery
Barry Egan, T.D
W B Yeats, Chairman
Leo MacAuley, M.A. B.L. of the Department of Finance, Secretary

1928

The tower

On 14 February 1928 *The tower* was published by Macmillan. The book opened with the most recently written poem, 'Sailing to Byzantium', first published in Cuala's *October blast* in 1927. Yeats's interest in Byzantium had been roused by his visit to Ravenna with Lady Gregory in 1907. In *A vision* he wrote, 'I think if I could be given a month of Antiquity and leave to spend it where I chose, I would spend it in Byzantium, a little before Justinian opened St. Sophia and closed the Academy of Plato.' In a talk for the BBC he claimed, 'Byzantium was the centre of European civilisation and the source of its spiritual philosophy, so I symbolise the search for the spiritual life by a journey to that city.' In April 1928, still recovering from illness, he wrote to a friend:

Re-reading THE TOWER I was astonished at its bitterness, and long to live out of Ireland that I may find some new vintage. Yet that bitterness gave the book its power and it is the best book I have written. Perhaps if I were in better health I should be content to be bitter.

Controversy over *The silver tassie*

In June 1928 Yeats found himself at the centre of another controversy over a play by Sean O'Casey. He had decided to reject for the Abbey O'Casey's latest play, *The silver tassie*, which dealt with Irish participation in World War I; letters explaining his reasons for rejecting it were inadvertently sent to O'Casey by Lady Gregory. Incensed at Yeats's comments, O'Casey then published the letters in the *Observer* newspaper. To defend himself, Yeats published more of the correspondence, and his rift with O'Casey was not made up for years. Later, Yeats wrote, 'When the directors of the Abbey Theatre rejected *The silver tassie* they did so because they thought it a bad play and a play which would mar the fame and popularity of its writer.' At the time, however, he had objected to it on the grounds that O'Casey had not himself participated in World War I, and that it lacked the unifying presence of one central hero.

After this rejection, O'Casey moved to Devon and remained in England for the rest of his life; his later plays did not enjoy the artistic or popular success of those written while he lived in Ireland.

MR. W. B. YEATS: "Of course, Mr. O'Casey, you must on no account take this as being in the nature of a rejection. I would suggest that you simply tell the Press that my foot slipped."

WBY rejecting *The silver tassie*

Book cover of *The tower* and manuscript of 'Sailing to Byzantium' (background and below)

page one hundred and thirty-nine

The silver tassie was performed at the Abbey in 1935, and caused more controversy, attracting condemnation from the clergy. It is now considered by many critics to be one of O'Casey's finest plays.

'Words for music perhaps'

Spring of 1929 was a particularly creative period for Yeats, during which he wrote the sequence of poems 'Words for music perhaps', influenced by his immersion in Jonathan Swift (1667–1745), the great Anglo-Irish satirist. He recorded later:

Life returned to me as an impression of the uncontrollable energy and daring of the great creators; it seemed to me that but for journalism and criticism, all that evasion and explanation, the world would be torn to pieces. I wrote 'Mad as the Mist and Snow', a mechanical little song, and after that all the group of songs called in memory of those exultant weeks 'Words for Music Perhaps.'

The poems, including the 'Crazy Jane' and 'Tom the lunatic' poems, were published in *Words for music perhaps and other poems* by Cuala in 1932.

Fighting the waves

On 13 August 1929 Yeats attended the first performance of *Fighting the waves*, a prose version of his play *The only jealousy of Emer*, at the Abbey. Also in attendance were the Governor General, the American Ambassador and other politicians. It was directed by Ninette de Valois, with music by George Antheil and masks by the Dutch ceramicist Hildo van Krop. Yeats was very impressed with the whole performance. In a letter to Olivia Shakespear he described it as his greatest success since *Cathleen ni Houlihan*.

II

On the afternoon of October 24th 1917, four days after my marriage, my wife surprised me by attempting automatic writing. What came in disjointed sentences, in almost illegible writing, was so exciting, sometimes so profound, that I persuaded her to give an hour or two day after day to the unknown writer, and after some half dozen such hours offered to spend what remained of life explaining and piecing together those scattered sentences. "No" was the answer, "we have come to give you metaphors for poetry". The unknown writer took his theme at first from my just published PER AMICA SILENTIA LUNAE. I had made a distinction between the perfection that is from a man's combat with himself and that which is from a combat with circumstance, and upon this simple distinction he built up an elaborate classification of men according to their more or less complete expression of one type or the other. He supported this classification by a series of geometrical symbols and put these symbols in an order that answered a question in my essay as to whether some prophet could not prick upon the calendar the birth of a Napoleon or a Christ. A system of symbolism, strange to my wife and to myself, awaited expression, and when I asked how long that would

I 2

take I was t
strays back
Browning's
until he had
ding of his B
Wilhelm M
another, and
histories.

When the a
hotel on the
turned to Ire
dalough, at I
near it, at Th

*see page 1
en 8*

of
certainly

page one hundred and forty-one

A packet for Ezra Pound

In August 1929 *A packet for Ezra Pound* was published by Cuala Press. This short book starts with an account of the Italian town of Rapallo and its inhabitants (who included Ezra Pound, playwright Gerhart Hauptmann, and composer George Antheil), which is followed by the poem 'Meditations upon death', written in February 1929 (now 'At Algeciras—a meditation upon death' and 'Mohini Chatterjee'). The essay 'Introduction to "The Great Wheel"' explains the origins of the material used in *A vision*, and Yeats was soon claiming that it would form the introduction to a revised version of *A vision*. However, 'Introduction to "The Great Wheel"' reveals a great deal about George's automatic writing and this caused a row between them. According to Yeats, it was the only serious row of their marriage. He later incorporated this material into the revised edition of *A vision*, in which he revealed still more about the automatic writing.

Rapallo

Arriving in Rapallo in November 1929, Yeats suffered a complete nervous collapse. By December his health had worsened and he made an emergency will witnessed by Ezra Pound and Basil Bunting. His illness was finally diagnosed as Malta fever (brucellosis) and his recovery was very slow. He continued his convalescence at Rapallo, nursed by George, and reading little but detective fiction and westerns.

430 Rapallo - Panotama e Golfo Tigullio

PART SIX: 1930–1939

THE GOLDEN SMITHIES OF THE EMPEROR

Miracle, bird or golden handiwork,
More miracle than bird or handiworak,
Planted on the star-lit golden bough,
Can like the cocks of Hades crow,
Or, by the moon embittered, scorn aloud
In glory of changeless metal
Common bird or petal
And all complexities of mire or blood.

BYZANTIUM

1930

The words upon the window pane

On 17 November 1930 Yeats's play *The words upon the window pane* was performed for the first time at the Abbey Theatre. The setting for the play is a séance in a house in Dublin. It combines Yeats's interests in Swift and spiritualism and reflects his political concerns of the time. The device by which Swift's words are mediated in the play by Mrs Henderson, a poor uneducated medium, epitomises Yeats's reaction to the democracy of the time: 'To me, mediumship is the antithesis of the highly developed, conscious individuality . . . you may even call it democracy in its final form.' Shortly after the first performance, Yeats began work on an introduction to *The words upon the window pane*, which was published in instalments in the *Dublin Magazine* between October 1931 and March 1932. In the introduction, he discussed the influence of Swift on his thinking and on his political ideas, and the second instalment caused some controversy.

John Masefield

On 5 November 1930 John Masefield organised a celebration to mark the thirtieth anniversary of his first meeting with Yeats. Yeats regularly attended performances of Masefield's plays in London, where they often met and dined together, and Yeats had dedicated his play *The cat and the moon* to Masefield. From his sickbed in Rapallo in May 1930, Yeats had written to Masefield to congratulate him on his appointment as poet laureate. Yeats persuaded him to act as a judge for the Harmsworth Prize in 1934, and it was Masefield who organised the memorial service for Yeats at Saint Martin-in-the-Fields in London in March 1939.

John Masefield

J.M. Synge

1931

Problems at Cuala Press

In May 1931 Yeats sold some of his stock in order to pay off debts at Cuala Press, and he also arranged to pay half of his sister Lily's salary (£92 per annum). The arrangement left Yeats and his wife short of money. Yeats's sisters and Cuala Industries suffered chronic financial problems. In 1923 he had paid £400 for Lily's convalescence at a London nursing home after the diagnosis of a serious illness. In 1924 he paid off £800 of Cuala's debts, and in 1925 paid off a further £2,000. Cuala Industries even moved into Yeats's home at 82 Merrion Square for two years before opening its showrooms on Baggot Street. By 1937 he had set about attempting to reorganise Cuala and decided to provide it with some controversial writing for publication that would increase its income. His plan materialised as the *Broadsides* and *On the boiler*.

1932

Death of Lady Gregory

From July to the end of 1931 Yeats spent much of his time at Coole Park with Lady Gregory, who was seriously ill with cancer. Lady Gregory's cancer had been diagnosed in 1923 and she was operated on then and again in 1926 and 1929. She regularly stayed with the Yeatses in Dublin, to deal with Abbey Theatre and Lane pictures business, and to convalesce after her operations. Accompanying her back to Coole after one operation, Yeats started writing the poem 'Coole Park, 1929' for Lady Gregory's memoir, *Coole*, published in 1931. During the summer and autumn of 1931 he wrote several poems, including 'The mother of God', 'The results of thought', 'Remorse for intemperate speech', and a number of sections of 'Words for music perhaps', Yeats continued to visit and stay at Coole through the early part of 1932, and arrived at Gort from Dublin on 23 May, only to hear that Lady Gregory had died earlier that morning. Writing to a friend, Yeats said that 'When she died the great house died too.' He attended her funeral two days later, and in the following years had difficult relations with the Gregory estate over publication of her diaries and letters.

Lady Gregory, pictured after the death of her son Robert

Jonathan Swift

Irish Academy of Letters

In September 1932 the Irish Academy of Letters held its first meeting. It had been established by Yeats and G.B. Shaw as part of an effort to combat censorship in Ireland after the introduction of the Censorship Bill of 1928. This infamous bill had arisen from a recommendation by the Evil Literature Committee, which Kevin O'Higgins had established in 1926, and was to have devastating consequences for Irish writers over the next 50 years, causing many of the best literary works to be banned. In March 1933 Yeats wrote to Ezra Pound:

Things are developing here into a devil of a fight. I have founded an Irish Academy, sufficient endowments have been found for it and all the clerical press is denouncing it, and some of the secular.

Riversdale

In 1932 the Yeatses moved into Riversdale in Rathfarnham, County Dublin, Yeats's last home in Ireland. He described the house and particularly the gardens in the last letter he wrote to Lady Gregory on 15 May 1932:

It is old, & has the most beautiful gardens I have seen round a small house—flower garden, fruit garden, vegetable garden, tennis & crockey [sic] lawns. A Mrs Nugent lived there till her death a short time ago, & created & tended the gardens for which she had a genius.

In June 1932, writing to Olivia Shakespear, he described it as having 'apple trees, cherry trees, roses, smooth lawns & no long climb upstairs'. In another letter in July he told her that George was painting the walls of his study yellow and the doors green and black, adding, 'we have a lease for but thirteen years but that [will] see me out of life'.

Riversdale, Rathfarnham, County Dublin.
Painting by Anne Yeats

1933

Eamon de Valera

At the beginning of March 1933 Yeats objected to the de Valera government's attempt to impose its candidate on the Board of Directors of the Abbey Theatre. The Minister for Finance had decided to appoint Professor William Magennis as the government's representative on the Abbey Board, and also complained of the programme of plays presented by the Abbey on its recent tour of America. Yeats wrote to the Minister on 1 March refusing the demand that they leave out certain plays on their American tours and refusing Magennis as a director. Yeats also stated the decision of the Board of Directors to refuse any further funding from the government. Writing to Ezra Pound a few days later, he said, 'The liberty of thought is very seriously threatened here.' Yeats had an hour-long interview with de Valera on 8 March to discuss the situation and wrote afterwards:

I had never met him before & I was impressed by his simplicity & honesty though we differed through out . . . I had gone there full of suspicion, but my suspicion vanished at once.

Blueshirts

In July 1933 Yeats met Eoin O'Duffy at Riversdale. O'Duffy had been dismissed from his post as police commissioner by de Valera in February, and in July became leader of the Fascist 'Blueshirts', who combined anti-communism and populist Catholicism. Yeats called their approach 'Fascism modified by religion'. In defiance of de Valera, O'Duffy proclaimed a new constitution and announced a march on Dublin by his Blueshirts. Yeats wrote:

Politics are growing hectic. De Valera has forced political thought to face the most fundamental issues. A Fascist opposition is forming behind the scenes to be ready should some tragic situation develop. I find myself constantly urging the despotic rule of the educated classes as the only end to our troubles . . . Our chosen colour is blue, & blue shirts are marching about all over the country . . . The chance of being shot is raising everybody's spirits enormously.

Eamon de Valera

Blueshirts

De Valera acted swiftly to ban the march, and O'Duffy's organisation dissipated gradually during the year. Yeats wrote 'Three songs to the same tune' for the Blueshirts in 1933, but in December 1938, a month before his death, he rewrote them as 'Three marching songs'.

The winding stair and other poems

On 19 September 1933 Macmillan published *The winding stair and other poems*. The volume collected poems previously published in *The winding stair*, published by Fountain Press in New York in 1928, and *Words for music perhaps and other poems*, published by Cuala Press in 1932. He wrote later that 'In this book and elsewhere I have used towers, and one tower in particular, as symbols and have compared their winding stairs to the philosophical gyres . . .' In Yeats's *A vision*, the gyres are two interpenetrating spirals in the form of cones, simultaneously winding and unwinding. Yeats put it thus:

If I call [one] *cone 'Discord' and the other 'Concord' and think of each as the bound of a gyre, I see that the gyre of 'Concord' diminishes as that of 'Discord' increases, and can imagine after that the gyre of 'Concord' increasing while that of 'Discord' diminishes, and so on, one gyre within the other always. Here the thought of Heraclitus dominates all: 'Dying each other's life, living each other's death.'*

Collected poems

On 14 November 1933 Yeats's *Collected poems* was published by Macmillan in New York, followed a fortnight later by an edition published by Macmillan in London. Yeats had begun discussing a seven-volume *edition de luxe* of his works with Macmillan late in 1930 but by March 1933 Macmillan decided to postpone this and agreed to publish a *Collected poems* and a *Collected plays* instead. The *Collected poems* was published in November 1933 and the

Book cover of
The winding stair

WBY broadcasting at
BBC, 1937

Collected plays in November 1934. Yeats continued to work towards an *edition de luxe*, making revisions to his essays and other works, but it was not to appear in his lifetime.

Steinach operation

In April 1934 Yeats underwent a Steinach operation or vasectomy. At the time the operation was considered to increase sexual prowess and slow down ageing. Norman Haire, who performed Yeats's operation, also administered a series of injections intended to increase sexual potency. The operation was considered a success, and perhaps its effects encouraged his subsequent affairs with Margot Ruddock and Ethel Mannin. In June 1935, at the height of his post-Steinach excitement, he wrote to Dorothy Wellesley:

I find my present weakness made worse by the strange second puberty the operation has given me, the ferment that has come upon my imagination. If I write more poetry it will be unlike anything I have done.

Margot Ruddock

At the end of August 1934 Yeats received a letter from Margot Ruddock, a young poet and admirer, who, although of course he did not know it at first, suffered from periodic bouts of mental illness. Within weeks, their correspondence was on an intimate level and by October he had organised a flat in London in order to conduct an affair with her. Yeats took an interest in her poetry, and tried to involve her in the work of the Group Theatre, a London theatre of the *avant garde* in which he was becoming interested. In 1936, while Yeats was recovering from serious illness in Majorca, she arrived in a fit of mania and had to be sent back to England in the care of a nurse at Yeats's expense. He wrote a preface for some poems of hers that were published in the *London Mercury* in July 1936 and she assisted him with a BBC broadcast in October 1937. This was the last time they met. By the end of 1937 Margot Ruddock had been committed to a mental institution, where she died some years later.

Margot Ruddock

Ethel Mannin

In December 1934 Yeats met the young writer Ethel Mannin at a party given by Norman Haire. Yeats and Mannin left the party together and returned to Mannin's apartment, where they established a lasting friendship. By late December he was writing to her as 'My dear O My dear' and telling her that the knowledge that he is not unfit for love has brought him sanity and peace. His sense of excitement is clear in a short note to Olivia Shakespear on 27 December: 'Are you back? Wonderful things have happened. This is Baghdad. This is not London.' Yeats met Mannin often in 1935, but by June she had met her future husband and her love affair with Yeats was over. However, they maintained a strong friendship and a lively correspondence until his death.

Group Theatre

In December 1934 Yeats attended meetings of the Group Theatre. The group involved included Rupert Doone, Ashley Dukes, T.S. Eliot and W.H. Auden, who planned to put on *avant garde* productions of poetic drama, including plays by Yeats. Yeats read *A full moon in March* to Doone in December 1934 but the Group Theatre never produced it. In 1935 Yeats heard Martin Browne lecture on T.S. Eliot's *Murder in the cathedral*, with verse spoken by Robert Speaight, and in November 1935 he saw Ashley Dukes's production of the play at the Mercury Theatre. Though the Group Theatre never produced any of Yeats's plays, his involvement brought him into contact with a younger generation of poets and poetic dramatists, and this encouraged his own poetic experimentation and his last plays.

WBY and T.S. Eliot

1935

Seventieth birthday

Yeats celebrated his seventieth birthday on 13 June 1935 with a small family meal at Riversdale, and again on 27 June with a banquet at the Royal Hibernian Hotel, hosted by the Irish branch of PEN (the International Association of Poets, Playwrights, Editors, Essayists, and Novelists). Poet Laureate John Masefield organised a committee of other writers and artists who presented Yeats with a drawing of Lucrezia Borgia by Dante Gabriel Rossetti. The *Irish Press* and the *Irish Times* printed articles about Yeats by friends and others, the *Irish Times* commenting:

From the national viewpoint W.B. Yeats occupies an almost unique position in Irish life; for he is virtually the first man since Swift who has been able to bring the Anglo-Irish tradition into line with a positive nationalism . . . He is Anglo-Irish and he is a Protestant. Yet there is no other Irishman of his day and generation who has done one tithe of his work for his native land.

In July, Harry Clifton, a rich aspiring poet friend of Oliver St John Gogarty's, presented Yeats with a piece of carved lapis lazuli that became one of his treasured possessions and the subject of the poem 'Lapis lazuli', written a year later.

Death of George Russell

On 17 July 1935 George Russell died of stomach cancer in Bournemouth. Yeats met the mail boat bearing Russell back to Ireland on 20 July and attended his state funeral, but refused to give the funeral oration. Writing to a friend, Yeats said:

All is well with AE. His ghost will not walk. He had no passionate human relationships to draw him back. My wife said the other night 'AE was the nearest to a saint you or I will ever meet. You are a better poet but no saint. I suppose one has to choose.'

p. 79   Proposed design by Edwin Lutyens, from the Hugh Lane Gallery.

p. 80   Abbey Theatre, from Fáilte Ireland.

p. 87   Maud Gonne and her children, Iseult Gonne and Sean MacBride, courtesy of Anna MacBride White.

p. 89   J. M. Synge, from Fáilte Ireland.

p. 95   Etta Wreidt, from the Mary Evans Picture Library.

p. 102   Hugh Lane: painting by John Singer Sargent, from the Hugh Lane Gallery.

p. 105   Mitchio Ito in *At the Hawk's Well*, from Reading University Library.

p. 109   Thoor Ballylee, from Fáilte Ireland.

p. 111   George Yeats with WBY in New York, from Getty Images.

p. 117   Lady Gregory's son Robert, from Colin Smythe.

p. 125   82 Merrion Square, from Fáilte Ireland.

p. 128   Sean O'Casey, from Fáilte Ireland.

p. 131   Ottoline Morrell, from the National Portrait Gallery.

p. 141   WBY at Garsington Manor, from the National Portrait Gallery.

p. 147   Lady Gregory, from Colin Smythe.

p. 151   Eamon de Valera: painting by Sir John Lavery, from Felix Rosenstiel's Widow and Son Ltd, courtesy of the Hugh Lane Gallery.

p. 157   WBY and T.S. Eliot, from Getty Images.

p. 165   Edith Shackleton Heald with WBY and Edmund Dulac, from the Huntington Library, San Marino, California.

p. 169   WBY with his dog, from Fáilte Ireland.

p. 171   Drumcliff churchyard, from Fáilte Ireland.

p. 174   WBY's tombstone at Drumcliff, from Fáilte Ireland.

Every effort has been made to establish contact with the holders of original copyright; in cases where this has not been possible we hope a general acknowledgement will be taken as sufficient.

SOURCES OF ILLUSTRATIONS

All illustrations are reproduced courtesy of Michael Yeats and the Board of the National Library of Ireland, with several exceptions. Where images are credited to other institutions, the copyright belongs to them and the images may not be reproduced without their express permission.

BIBLIOGRAPHY

Brown, Terence (1999) *The life of W.B. Yeats*. Dublin: Gill and Macmillan.

Clark, David R. and Rosalind E. Clark (1987) 'Sailing from Avalon: Yeats's first play, *Vivien and time*, in Richard Finneran (ed.), *Yeats: an annual of critical and textual studies*, *vol. v*. London: Macmillan.

Eliot, T.S. (1975) *Selected prose*. Frank Kermode, ed. London: Faber and Faber.

Ellmann, Richard (1949) *Yeats: the man and the masks*. London: Macmillan.

Finneran, Richard (ed.) (1983) *The collected poems of W.B. Yeats*. London: Macmillan.

Foster, R.F. (1998) *W.B. Yeats: a life, vol. i: the apprentice mage, 1865–1914*. Oxford University Press.

— (2003) *W.B. Yeats: a life, vol. ii: the arch poet, 1915–1939*. Oxford University Press.

Kelly, John S. (2003) *A W.B. Yeats chronology*. Basingstoke: Palgrave Macmillan.

— (ed.) (1986, 1994, 2005) *The collected letters of W.B. Yeats, vols i–iv*. Oxford University Press.

— (ed.) *The collected letters of W.B. Yeats*. InteLex past masters electronic edition. (www.library.nlx.com).

Kiberd, Declan (1995) *Inventing Ireland*. London: Jonathan Cape.

Murphy, W.M. (1995) *Family secrets: William Butler Yeats and his relatives*. Dublin: Gill and Macmillan.

Yeats, William Butler (1926) *Autobiographies: reveries over childhood and youth and the trembling of the veil*. London: Macmillan.

Cast a cold Eye
On Life, on Death,
Horseman pass by!

W.B. YEATS

June 13th 1865
January 24th 1939

WBY's funeral in Drumcliff
churchyard, County Sligo

Manuscript of 'Under
Ben Bulben' (opposite)

London in March. On 6 September 1948 Yeats's bones were removed in state from Roquebrune to Nice, and then brought to Sligo on the Irish Navy's ship, *Macha*. It arrived on 17 September to be met by George, Michael, Anne and Jack Yeats, and was accompanied by a military guard of honour to the cemetery at Drumcliff where Yeats's remains were reinterred according to his wishes. Seán MacBride (son of Maud Gonne and Minister for External Affairs, closely involved in the organisation of the repatriation), Edith Shackleton Heald and Louis MacNeice were among those present at the funeral.

Last poems and two plays

On 10 July 1939 Cuala Press published Yeats's *Last poems and two plays*. Four of the poems ('The statues', 'News for the Delphic Oracle', 'Long-legged fly' and 'A bronze head') had appeared in the March issue of the *London Mercury*, and others had appeared in issues of the *New Republic* in February and March 1939. The book also contained the poems Yeats was working on at the time of his death ('The black tower' and 'Cuchulain comforted') as well as the play *The death of Cuchulain*, which he had been revising on his deathbed, and *Purgatory*, which had been performed in August 1938. Yeats had been working on the arrangement of the contents of the book at the time of his death, and had placed 'Under Ben Bulben' first so that the following poems seem to come from the grave. The ordering of the poems was changed for the Macmillan edition, *Last poems & plays*, published in 1940.

Drumcliff churchyard with Ben Bulben in background

WBY's grave at Roquebrune

WBY's remains being brought by boat from France

To Edith Shackleton Heald he described it as a strange play and 'the most moving I have written for some time'. He added, 'I am making the prose sketch for a poem—a kind of sequel— strange too, something new.' This poem became 'Cuchulain comforted'. Yeats continued to dictate corrections to the manuscript of *The death of Cuchulain* on 22 and 26 January and, after his death, George gave the manuscript to Dorothy Wellesley. The play had its first performance at the Abbey Theatre on 13 August 1949.

'Under Ben Bulben'

Early in August 1938 Yeats wrote his epitaph and began work on the poem that became 'Under Ben Bulben'.

In a letter to Dorothy Wellesley on 15 August 1938, Yeats claimed his epitaph was influenced by reading Rainer Maria Rilke's ideas on death. In this version and some of the other early drafts, the epitaph starts with the line, 'Draw rein, draw breath.' This line, however, was dropped from subsequent drafts. In the early drafts, Yeats started the poem with the line, 'I believe what the old saints . . .' and called it 'Creed'. Later he changed this title to 'His convictions'. He finished writing it on 4 September 1938 but dictated some changes on 26 January 1939, two days before his death. At that stage he changed the title to 'Under Ben Bulben'.

Death and burial

At 2.30 p.m. on Saturday 28 January 1939, Yeats died at the Hôtel Idéal-Séjour, Cap Martin, after which Edith Shackleton Heald and George Yeats kept vigil over the body. On Sunday 29 January the body was removed to the cemetery chapel at Roquebrune, where he was buried at 3 p.m. on Monday 30 January according to the Anglican rite. George Yeats, Dorothy Wellesley, Edith Shackleton Heald, Hilda Matheson, and Mabel and Dermod O'Brien attended as mourners. On 3 February George had the poem 'Under Ben Bulben' published in three Dublin newspapers to forestall calls for a Dublin burial. Memorial services were held in Dublin in February and in

THE DEATH OF CUCHULAIN.

(A bare stage of any period. A very old man looking like something out of mythology.)

MAN: I have been asked to produce a play called "The Death of Cuchullain". It is the last of a series of plays which has for theme his life and death. I have been selected because I am out of fashion and out of date like the antiquated romantic stuff the thing is made of. I am so old that I have forgotten the name of my father and mother, unless indeed I am, as I affirm, the of Talma, and he was so old that his friend acquaintances still read Virgil and Homer. they told me that I could have my own way certain guiding principles on a bit of ne I wanted an audience of fifty or a hundre if there are more, I beg them not to shur feet or talk when the actors are speakin sure that as I am producing a play for p

WBY at home with his dog

Manuscript and proofs of *The death of Cuchulain*

'A bronze head' was one of four poems by Yeats published after his death in the *London Mercury* in March 1939.

Purgatory

On 15 March 1938, Yeats wrote to Edith Shackleton Heald that he had an idea for a new play that became *Purgatory*:

I have a one-act play in my head, a scene of tragic intensity . . . I am so afraid of that dream. My recent work has greater strangeness and I think greater intensity than anything I have done.

Yeats worked on *Purgatory* on his arrival in Steyning at the end of March. The first performance took place in August at the Abbey Theatre with designs by his daughter Anne. The play is set at the ruins of a great house beside a bare tree, both symbolic of the play's central concern, the decline of an aristocratic family as a result of miscegenation and degeneration. *Purgatory* was published in *On the boiler* in the autumn of 1939 with a collection of essays on social politics.

The death of Cuchulain

In March 1938, while staying with Edith Shackleton Heald, Yeats began work on *The death of Cuchulain*, completing a draft version by May. On 20 October 1938 he wrote to Ethel Mannin:

I am writing a play on the death of Cuchulain, an episode or two from the old epic. My 'private philosophy' is there but there must [be] no sign of it . . . To me all things are made of the conflict of two states of consciousness, beings or persons which die each other's life, live each other's death. That is true of life and death themselves. Two cones (or whirls) the apex of each in the other's base.

Maud Gonne
in old age

A vision

The heavily revised second edition of *A vision* was published on 7 October 1937. Yeats had begun revising it as early as 1927, less than two years after the publication of the first edition, and he continued working on revisions intermittently, though the second edition had been largely ready since 1931 and held up by Macmillan's lack of enthusiasm. The second edition incorporated *A packet for Ezra Pound*, first published in 1929, revealing George Yeats's automatic writing, and using the *Stories of Michael Robartes and his friends* (Cuala, 1931) to contain the narrative of the discovery of Giraldus's book and to provide an absurdist prologue to the occult material.

The revisions bring the spiritual aspects of the system further forward and treat the afterlife more fully than in the first version, but the system resolutely retains its emphasis on the individualistic, subjective human. Traditional spirituality and Christianity are associated with the objective unifying force (the *primary*); Yeats casts himself as the representative and advocate of the subjective separating force (the *antithetical*) and he predicts an imminent change to a new more individualistic form of religion.

1938

'A bronze head'

In February 1938 Yeats was writing the poem 'A bronze head.' The poem was prompted by a bronze-painted plaster cast of Maud Gonne by Laurence Campbell that Yeats saw at the Municipal Gallery of Modern Art in Dublin. At this time, Maud Gonne habitually dressed in black and was frequently seen at political funerals. Yeats contrasted this 'dark tomb-haunter' with the light, gentle woman he had once known, and this led him to reflect on change and decay. In August 1938 he met Maud Gonne for the last time and told her that they should have gone ahead with their plans for a Castle of the Heroes, and that they still might. In October 1938 Yeats read and was upset by Maud Gonne's autobiography, *A servant of the Queen*. He wrote to his wife, saying:

Read much of Maud's book last night—sufficiently upset by it to have a not very good night.
Very much herself always—remarkable intellect at the service of the will, no will at the service
of the intellect.

NO. 5 (NEW SERIES) MAY 1935.

A BROADSIDE

EDITORS: W. B. YEATS AND F. R. HIGGINS; MUSICAL EDITOR,
ARTHUR DUFF. PUBLISHED MONTHLY AT THE CUALA PRESS,
ONE HUNDRED AND THIRTY THREE LOWER BAGGOT STREET,
DUBLIN.

THE ROSE TREE
"O words are lightly spoken,"
Said Pearse to Connolly,
"Some politicians idle words
Have withered our Rose Tree;
Or maybe but a wind that blows
Across the bitter sea."

300 copies only.

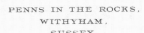

PENNS IN THE ROCKS,
WITHYHAM,
SUSSEX.

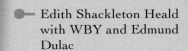

Edith Shackleton Heald
with WBY and Edmund
Dulac

Oxford book of modern verse

In 1934 Yeats was invited by Oxford University Press to edit a volume of modern poetry. He immersed himself in books of poetry by many of the new young poets as well as many of the established ones already known to him. The collection championed some of his personal favourites and his very subjective selection caused controversy when the book was published in November 1936. As had often happened in Yeats's life, the controversy helped boost sales, and 15,000 copies were sold in the first three months. This provided him with much needed income as well as bringing him to public attention again. In October 1936, just weeks before the book's publication, the BBC broadcast Yeats's talk on modern poetry which was based on his introduction to the *Oxford book of modern verse*.

1937

Edith Shackleton Heald

In April 1937 Yeats was introduced to journalist and editor Edith Shackleton Heald, with whom he began an intimate friendship. After their first meeting he sent her a copy of his lectures as a tribute, and by June 1937 she was driving him to and from her house at Steyning in Sussex where Yeats spent much of his time in 1938. Her house was close to the registry office where Parnell had married Katherine O'Shea in 1891. Edith Shackleton Heald travelled with Yeats and was among those present at his deathbed in 1939.

Broadsides

The first series of *Broadsides* was published in 1935 by Cuala Press and included works by Yeats, James Stephens, F.R. Higgins, Frank O'Connor, Lynn Doyle, Bryan Guinness and Padraic Colum, and illustrations by Jack Yeats, Harry Kernoff, Sean O'Sullivan and Maurice McGonigal, among others.

THE EUGENICS SOCIETY

Telephone : VICtoria, 7302
Cables and Wires :
" Heredity (Sowest) London."
(Two Words)

President
THE LORD HORDER, K.C.V.O., M.D., F.R.C.P.

General Secretary
C. P. BLACKER, M.C., M.A., M.D., F.R.C.P.
CPB/PP

69 Eccleston Square,
London, S.W.1

17th January, 1938.

W.B.Yeats, Esq..
Terminus Hotel,
Monte Carlo.

Dear Mr. Yeats,

Thank you for your letter of January 13th. I
I know of no observations as to intelligence quotients
among the leisured classes living on unearned incomes.
Such persons would be very difficult to get hold of
in any organised body.

Yours sincerely,

Blacker

ON THE BOILER

By

W. B. YEATS

THE CUALA PRESS · DUBLIN

PRICE : THREE SHILLINGS AND SIXPENCE

EUGENICS SOCIETY

FIXTURES, AUTUMN 1938.

At the Rooms of the ROYAL SOCIETY, Burlington House, Piccadilly, W.1. (by kind permission of the President and Council of the Royal Society.)

TUESDAY, OCTOBER 18TH. at 5.15 p.m.

Intelligence and Family Size.

Speaker : J. A. FRASER ROBERTS, M.B., D.Sc., F.R.S.E.

TUESDAY, NOVEMBER 15TH at 5.15 p.m.

Intelligence Tests.

Speaker : PROFESSOR C. SPEARMAN, Ph.D., LL.D., F.R.S.

TUESDAY, DECEMBER 20TH at 5.15 p.m.

External Migration.

Speaker : R. S. WALSHAW.

All interested in the above subjects are invited to attend.
Tea will be provided at 4.45 p.m.

📍 Eugenics Society
fixtures list

🔴 Eugenics Society letter

🔴— WBY with his
brother Jack B.
Yeats (opposite)

page one hundred and sixty-three

Majorca

Shortly after his arrival in Majorca in December 1935, Yeats fell ill. George arrived in Majorca in February 1936 when he was suffering from nephritis and breathing difficulties. His imminent death was forecast in the London newspapers, but he made a slow recovery, putting on ordinary clothes in April for the first time since January. In August he suffered a relapse and his doctors administered digitalis, and prescribed a diet of milk and fruit.

Eugenics

Yeats applied for membership of the Eugenics Society as early as November 1936, and renewed his subscription in December 1937. While writing *On the boiler*, Yeats wrote to the Society seeking advice for articles he was working on. On a visit to Oxford in May 1938 he shocked guests at a dinner at All Souls with his eugenicist views on the excessive fertility of the proletariat. Yeats found evidence to support his eugenicist views everywhere—including the Abbey, where he claimed young Dublin actors had misshapen bodies compared with the older, country-bred actors. In *On the boiler*—which he intended to be provocative—he wrote:

Since about 1900 the better stocks have not been replacing their numbers, while the stupider and less healthy have been more than replacing theirs . . . One nation has solved the problem in its chief city; in Stockholm all families are small, but the greater the intelligence the larger the family.

Race, the degeneration of civilisation, and miscegenation become significant themes in his poetry around this time, and appear explicitly in works such as the play *Purgatory* and the poem 'The statues'.

Dorothy Wellesley.
Drawing by Sir
William Rothenstein

Shri Purohit Swami with
WBY

Rapallo, Italy

Book cover of *The Oxford*
book of modern verse

THE
OXFORD BOOK
OF
MODERN VERSE

THE GOLDEN SMITHIES OF THE EMPEROR

The spectacle of Russell's funeral set Yeats thinking about his own. By 1938 he had decided against a large Dublin funeral, saying that 'I write my poems for the Irish people but I am damned if I will have them at my funeral. A Dublin funeral is something between a public demonstration & a private picnic.' By then he was working on 'Under Ben Bulben'.

Dorothy Wellesley

Yeats met Dorothy Wellesley, wife of Lord Gerald Wellesley (later Seventh Duke of Wellington), for the first time in June 1935, when Ottoline Morrell drove him to Wellesley's romantic house at Penns in the Rocks, near Withyham on the Sussex–Kent border. He had read some of her poetry when he was editing the *Oxford book of modern verse*, and at their first meeting he told her, 'You must sacrifice everything and everyone to your poetry.' Yeats became a frequent visitor to Wellesley's home, editing and revising her poems as well as paying attention to her comments on his own works. Yeats provided the introduction for *Selections from the poems of Dorothy Wellesley*, published in June 1936. Together they edited the second series of *Broadsides* in 1937, and Wellesley and her partner Hilda Matheson were among those present at Yeats's deathbed in 1939. Matheson, who worked for the BBC, introduced Yeats to George Barnes, who produced several of his radio broadcasts.

Shri Purohit Swami

In December 1935 Yeats arrived in Majorca with Shri Purohit Swami, where they were to work on translations from the *Upanishads*. He had met the Swami through Sturge Moore and Olivia Shakespear. Yeats read part of the Swami's autobiography, *An Indian monk*, in 1932 and wrote an introduction for its publication by Macmillan. In October 1934 he wrote an introduction for some of the Swami's translations, which appeared in *Criterion*. Yeats restarted the translations while recovering from his illness in March 1936 and *The ten principal Upanishads* was published by Faber and Faber in April 1937. Faber also published *The aphorisms of yoga* in 1938 with an Introduction by Yeats and commentary by the Swami.

WILLIAM BUTLER YEATS

Aetat. 70

Dublin University League of Nations Society met a
...et in the College Park yesterday.

P.E.N. Club, at the Royal Hibernian Hotel, Dublin, last night, to Dr. W. B. Yeat...
...ul, Major P. Ruzicka, chatting with the guest of the evening. Centre: The Earl...
...he former and present Ministers for Finance enjoy a joke. Senator Ernest Blythe...
guests.

IRISH P. E. N.

W. B. YEATS
BIRTHDAY
DINNER

Royal Hibernian Hotel
27th June, 1935

*For life moves out of a red flare of dreams
Into a common light of common hours
Until old age bring the red flare again.*

- WBY and Major P. Ruzicka in the Royal Hibernian Hotel, Dublin

- Menu from WBY's seventieth birthday celebrations at the Royal Hibernian Hotel

- Seventieth birthday supplement in the *Irish Times*